ANTS

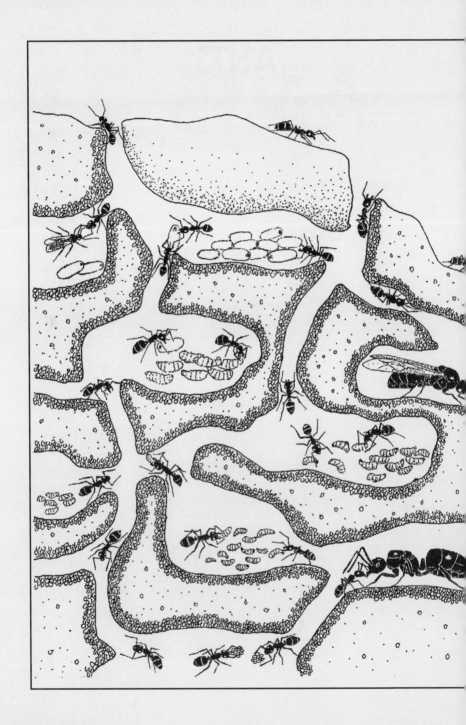

ANTS

Ray North

**WITH ILLUSTRATIONS BY GEOFF ALLEN
AND CARTOONS BY NICHOLAS PIKE**

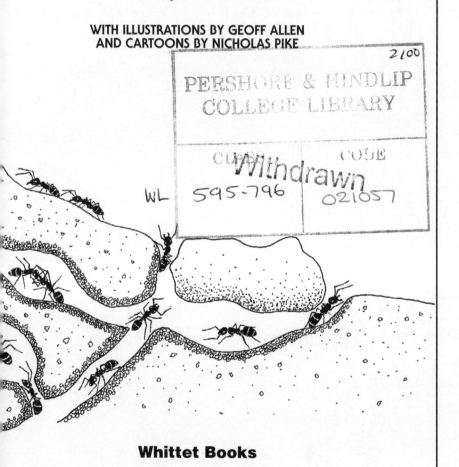

Whittet Books

TITLE PAGE ILLUSTRATION: *cutaway of black garden ant nest*

First published 1996
Text ©1996 by Ray North
Illustrations ©1996 by Geoff Allen
Cartoons ©1996 Nicholas Pike
Whittet Books Ltd, 18 Anley Road, London W14 OBY

Cataloguing in publication data
A catalogue record for this book is available from the British Library.

ISBN 1 873580 25 8

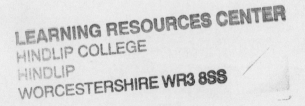
Printed and bound by Biddles of Guildford

Contents

Dinoponera

Introduction to ants

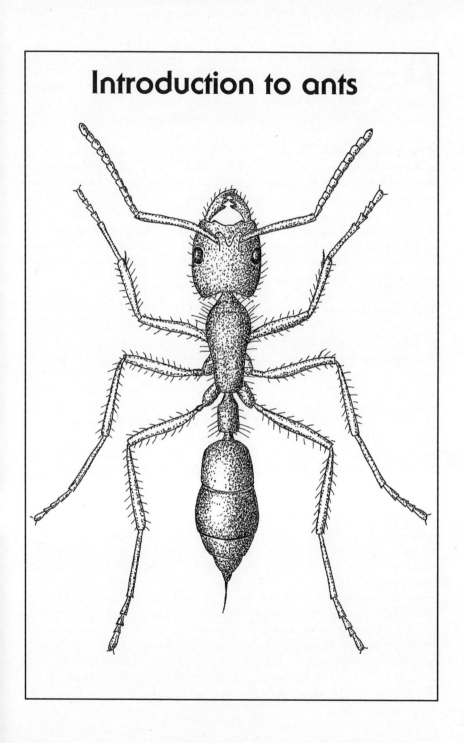

Ants are the most diverse of all social insects, the differences between species being seen in their body structure and behaviour; and it is ant behaviour that has so fascinated people (myrmecologist is the name of those who study ants) for over a century – their highly organised social structure, their altruism, their exploitation of other species.

What is a social insect?

Like bees and wasps, ants are social insects; but what is a social insect? As the word implies they are insects that live in a community; the famous American entomologist Edward Wilson set out certain criteria for insects to qualify as social insects: (i) there must be co-operation between individuals in rearing the young (ii) the actual act of reproducing must be carried out by a separate male and female caste (iii) at least two generations must overlap so that the offspring eventually help the parents to care for the young. Being a social insect is all down to team work.

Relatives of ants

Bees, ants and wasps belong to a large group or order of insects: Hymenoptera. The group also includes the lesser-known insects such as the ichneumon flies, sawflies, chalcid wasps, wood wasps and many parasitic species. The main characteristic feature of insects included in the Hymenoptera is that winged forms have two pairs of membranous wings. The fore wings and the smaller hind wings are held together by tiny hooks and work as a single unit. The ants are separated from bees and wasps by certain structural differences: ants have a long waist between the thorax and abdomen known as the petiole. The waist may have one or two segments depending on the species. Bees and wasps on the other hand do not have such a prominent petiole; owing to this difference in structure ants are given a family of their own, the Formicidae.

Termites are sometimes called 'white ants'. This is in fact a total misconception because termites are not ants, they are not even related to ants. They belong to a different order (Isoptera) which are closely related to cockroaches! There are of course similarities between them, the most important being that they are both social insects; even some features of their life cycles are alike. However, termites, unlike ants, have a king and queen which stay together after mating, whereas in ants the males die. Termite eggs do not hatch into grubs, as in ants, but into young workers that are tiny replicas of the adults. Another important difference between ants and termites is that the worker caste of ants are all female while termite societies have both male and female workers. As termites and ants are very different in many ways, considering the evolution of insects, socialisation has obviously evolved more than once.

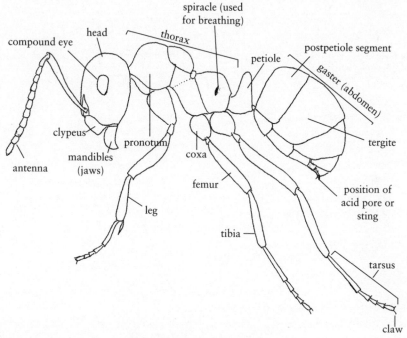

General structure of a worker ant

Types of ants

There are some 8,800 known species of ants in the world, and probably more to be discovered: it has been calculated that there may be as many as 20,000 species. The Formicidae is a large group, divided further into sub-families as illustrated in the ant family tree (overleaf). To make matters more complex each subfamily is divided into tribes, then genera, species and some-times a subspecies (genus and species are always written in italic print). A word about scientific names: all species, plant and animal, have two Latin names to avoid confusion so that scientists know exactly what species they are talking about. The first Latin name is the genus and the second the spe-cies, the genus name always starts with a capital and the species name with a small letter, e.g. *Formica rufa*. This is in fact a wood ant of which there are several different species within the genus *Formica*. I will where possible use the common names for the ants described but some do not have common names so I have no alternative but to use the Latin names.

I will briefly introduce the most important subfamilies to the reader, who will meet them throughout the book. Note that subfamily names always end in *nae*. The ant family tree shows that there are two major groupings of ants: on the left, the Poneroid complex, which includes primitive species, and on

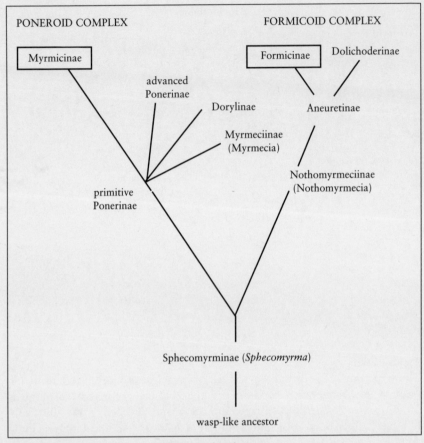

PONEROID COMPLEX   FORMICOID COMPLEX

The ant family tree

the right advanced species of the Formicoid complex. Primitive ants are those species that show body structures and behaviour very similar to that of their ancestors. Advanced species have more complex body structures and behaviour, so are reckoned to have improved on their ancestors.

I will mention now only the most important subfamily groups as some contain just one, or a few species. The Poneroid complex includes the advanced ponerinae (e.g. *Pogonomyrmex*) and the primitive ponerinae (e.g. *Amblypone*). The ponerinae are large carnivorous ants in which some species raid the nests of termites, on which they feed. The Myrmeciinae (*Myrmecia*) are known as the bull or jumping ants; they are native of Australia and New Guinea. Some species are very large, reaching 36 mm in

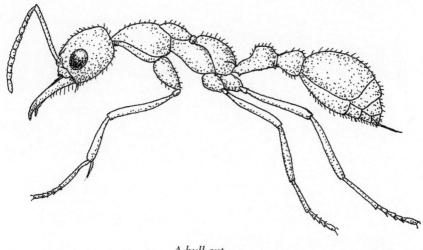

A bull ant

length and look a bit like wasps; their bright colouring may be an indication of their very painful sting. When the nest is disturbed the workers of this agile ant come springing out of the nest – they can jump up to a foot. Even more primitive than the bull ant is *Nothomyrmecia*, which is the most primitive of the Myrmeciinae. Myrmeciinae share similar behaviour patterns with the primitive ponerinae, *Amblypone*, such as the method of founding a new colony: in both cases a solitary queen founds a colony, caring for the young and foraging herself to bring back food for the larvae; yet structurally the two species are very different.

The Dorylinae includes the army and driver ants of South America and Africa respectively; these are nomadic ants that get their food by raiding. Their prey consists of a variety of invertebrate animals and sometimes small vertebrates. The Myrmicinae are a very large group as they include both tropical and temperate species. The red garden ants (*Myrmica*) found in Britain are part of this subfamily as well as important pest species like seed harvesting ants (*Messor*) and leaf-cutting ants (*Atta*), which use the leaves they cut to cultivate a fungus garden under the ground. Included also are the fire ants (*Solenopsis*), whose nasty sting causes humans to experience a burning sensation. I will elaborate all of these in more detail in later sections.

The Dolichoderinae are part of the Formicoid complex, and link some of the primitive ants with modern ants. Although some species may be quite large (1 centimetre/.5 inch in length) they have no sting but have evolved a good chemical defence system producing a variety of chemical substances from the anal region. The Formicinae, whose sting has been replaced by a

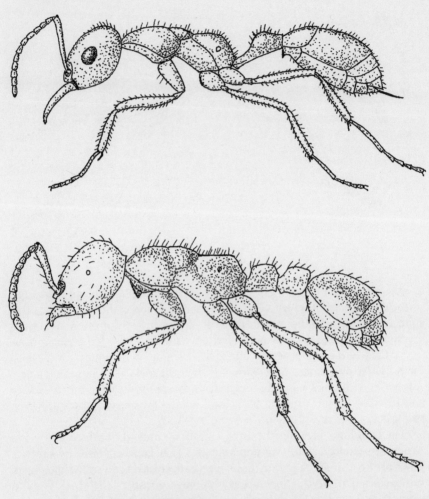

The most primitive ants alive today:
Nothomyrmecia *(above) and* Amblypone *(below)*

circular pore in the anal region called the acid pore, are the most advanced. The acid pore is particularly well developed in wood ants and is capable of firing a jet of formic acid at enemies. The crop of the Formicinae functions as a food storage organ and is well developed for the transportation of large volumes of that important ant food – honey-dew collected from aphids. The Formicinae also include, to mention but a few, the familiar black garden ants (*Lasius*), carpenter ants (*Camponotus*) and weaver ants (*Oecophylla*).

Ants world wide

Ants are found just about everywhere in the world. Being the only social predators in the soil gives them an advantage, for sociability means organisation and organisation, as humans know, means strength. However, many make their homes in trees and other types of vegetation. Ants are able to live in some of the most inhospitable environments – from the subarctic conditions of the Russian tundra to the hottest deserts of the world. In the subarctic they hibernate during the winter when their nests become full of ice crystals, surviving temperatures down to –40° C. These ants do not freeze because they accumulate antifreeze in their blood. About 14 species of ants can be found at the tree line in Northern Eurasia and America, some live about 50 miles (80 km) north of the tree line on Richard's Island.

Species that live in deserts nest underground and come out mainly at night. There are species that forage during the day but they tend to return to the nest around noon. One ant (*Cataglyphis*) is unusual in that it scavenges for food during the hottest part of the day. It makes frequent trips from its nest and is able to run very fast, as if on tip-toe, across the burning sand.

Many species are unique to certain continents, like the leaf-cutting ants and army ants (*Eciton* sp.) of South America, driver ants (*Dorylus* sp.) of Africa, or the Australian bull ants. In Britain and Europe, most people are familiar with common garden ants (red and black ants) and wood ants of woodlands and forests. These are temperate species living in the northern hemisphere, which includes North America. Temperate regions are generally poor in species of ants compared to the tropics; approximately 760 species compared to 6,700. The British Isles alone has about 42 species of ants.

Secrets of ant success

There are several reasons why ants are successful as social insects. Most important is their very efficient communication system based on chemicals known as pheromones. By releasing pheromones ants are able to tell nest mates of the whereabouts of food or warn them of impeding danger. To protect the colony and to aid them in their hunting, ants have an elaborate armoury of stings and chemical weapons. The jaws, which are very useful tools for cutting and grinding food, are also used both in defence and offence.

Individual workers carry out only a small number of tasks at any one time, therefore fewer mistakes are made. (Rather like working on a production line.) Some individuals are involved in reproduction, others in feeding and grooming brood, others in foraging for food, and yet others in guard duties or nest construction. Ants are unique in that they have evolved a special gland (metapleural gland) which produces antibiotic substances that inhibit the growth of micro-organisms in the moist nest chambers. Since they pile their eggs and larvae on bare soil inside a brood chamber, the licking of the eggs and larvae by ants removes micro-organisms and probably spreads antibiotic substances over the brood. In contrast, wasps and bees must build special brood cells (honeycomb structures) which are impregnated with antibiotics produced by their own glands.

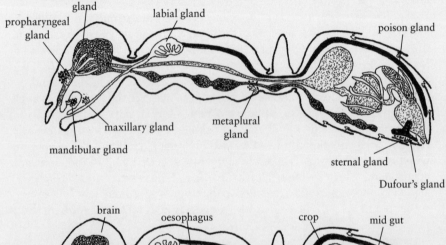

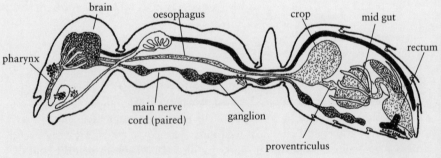

Internal anatomy of a worker ant showing the locations of various internal structures (below) and glands (above)

DINOSAUR ANTS

In Peru lives an ant with the scientific name of *Dinoponera longipes* or dino-saur ant which may reach 3 cm (1.2 in) or more in body length. Despite their name the workers are quite timid and soon hide beneath the leaf litter when approached. They are rather interesting because they have no queen as such, future generations are born of workers inseminated by males. What's more it seems that before brood can be reared successfully they must be fed on verte-brate prey. This includes baby mice (pinkies), birds, frogs and reptiles. Pinkie mice are dismembered slowly over about two days, even the bones are re-moved and chewed up! The workers hunt mainly at night, biting small live prey first and then stinging. The jaws then cut into the prey like the blade of a saw with back and forth movements of the head.

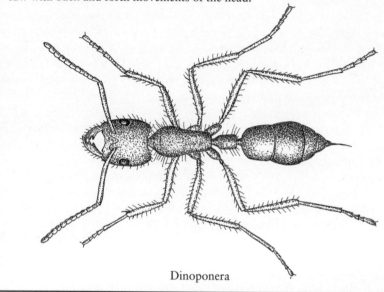

Dinoponera

Ant-cestry

About 65 million years ago species of ants began to multiply and adapt to different ways of life; many species evolved independently, giving rise to species of ants that are unique to the Old and New Worlds. The ancestors of ants are thought to be wasps; of the present day wasps the closest living relatives are the Tiphiidae, which are non–social wasps. Evidence for the wasp ancestors of ants comes from fossils which have enabled scientists to study the structural similarities between fossil forms and living ants and wasps of today. Whole specimens of fossil ants have been discovered preserved in amber. The most important fossil ant was found by Edward Wilson embedded in amber from New Jersey (USA). The specimen is estimated to be around 80 million years old and given the scientific name of *Sphecomyrma freyi*. It would have been alive with the dinosaurs during the Cretaceous period (136–64 million years ago). The dinosaurs became extinct at the end of this period. *Sphecomyrma freyi* is considered to be an important link between the ants of today and the non-social wasps. It shows several structural intermediate characteristics between ants and wasps: its waist or petiole is thin and jaws are like those of wasps (small with only two teeth). This posed a problem because *Amblypone,* which is one of the most primitive ants, has a broad petiole. We would have expected *Sphecomyrma* to have a waist similar to *Amblypone.* Maybe *Amblypone* evolved from a species that came before *Sphecomyrma*? We are still uncertain. Recent evidence shows that *Nothomyrmecia* is very similar to *Sphecomyrma* in body structure and *Amblypone* is like the advanced ponerinae in body structure, so two groups could have evolved from *Sphecomyrma* forming the Poneroid complex on one hand and the Formicoid complex on the other. However, the important link with modern ants is that *Sphecomyrma* has a metapleural gland (involved in the production of antibiotic substances mentioned above) which is peculiar to ants.

Sphecomyrma was probably fully social, having queens and workers. The evolution of social behaviour in ants was likely to have been a gradual process; the ants of today that we regard as 'primitive' because of their body structure are more solitary, and the ant fossil remains have all been individuals, with no brood or larvae near them. Socialisation may have started with the wasp-like ancestors: sister females (young queens) may have started to co-operate in nest building and transporting prey to larvae on which both the queens and larvae fed. As evolution progressed dominant and subordinate queens appeared, and the subordinate queens probably became workers. This could have led to the physical caste structure seen in ants of today. These evolutionary steps towards socialisation may be seen in some primitive wasps and ants alive today. The primitive paper wasps (*Polistes),* which are present world wide, including Britain, found nests as small groups of queens but in the end one queen will dominate. The primitive ant, *Nothomyrmecia,* begins a new colony with more than one queen and soon after subordinate queens are dragged out of the nest! Many primitive species of ants place their larvae on the prey rather than bringing the prey to the larvae; could this represent the beginnings of prey transportation? Moving prey or larvae to prey is important because it indicates the next stage in the evolution to advanced ants. The advanced species have perfected prey transportation; foragers carry prey to the nest, where it is fed to nurse workers who in turn regugitate food to the larvae. In spite of the similarities there is a very big gap indeed, in terms social behaviour, between the closest living relatives of the ants (among the wasps) and the most primitive living ants.

In this book I will take the reader through the fascinating world of ants explaining how a society of ants functions, how they obtain food, defend themselves and have adapted to live almost anywhere. The reader may find several similarities between ants and humans, particularly as man and ants are the only animals that wage war on their own species. The communication system of ants enables them to dominate the habitat in which they live, and in some cases that of humans too, when ants become serious agricultural pests. Ants play an important role in the environment and I will discuss the need for their conservation and their habitats in the final section in the book.

SOME LIKE IT HOT

Ants are actually 'thermophilic' insects, that is, they like warmth. But in the central desert of Australia lives a species of ant (*Melophorus bagoti*) that has taken this to the extreme. For this ant forages during the hottest part of the day when temperatures at the surface of the soil exceed 70°C.

Around midday, under a clear blue sky with air temperatures above 50°C, the workers are fully active while most other animals stay at home. However, this ant is not quite as foolish as it may first appear because at the hottest time of the day there is no competition for food as it is just too hot for other species to forage. *Melophorus* seems to love the heat. The workers are exposed to the sun for at least 10 seconds before they retreat to shade cast by sparse vegetation. It likes the heat so much that it will not start to search for food until the ground temperature reaches 56°C. During the spring when the temperature is around 52°C the numbers of ants seen outside the nest fall by 90%.

Clearly, these ants have special adaptations to enable them to survive such high temperatures. The body covering is impregnated with waxy or lipid materials which prevent the ants from drying out. They also have special proteins which do not denature at high temperatures; in contrast our own body proteins start to denature around 42°C!

Ant society

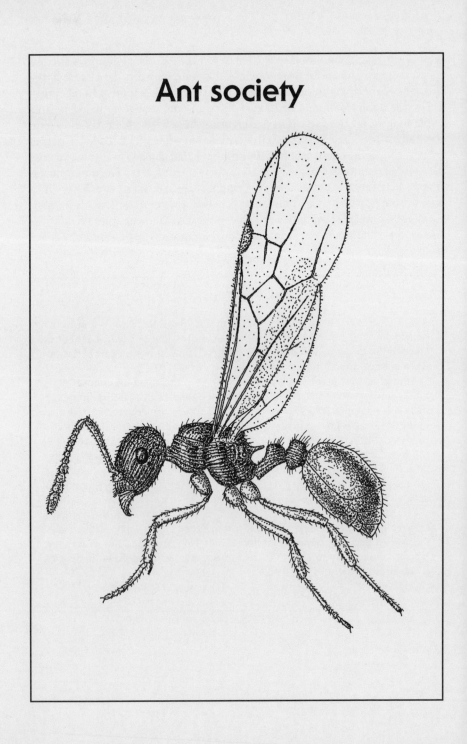

A nt society is made up of **worker ants,** which are all sterile females whose function in the community is to forage for food, defend the nest, rear the brood, construct or repair the nest, and take dead ants and other rubbish to a refuse pile outside the nest. A **queen ant** is responsible for laying eggs. The eggs hatch into grubs or larvae which develop into either workers, **young queens (gynes)** or **male** ants. Some ant societies have more than queen, while others have only one. The number of queens usually depends on the species of ant. Bee and wasp societies are very similar to ants in having a queen and workers; in bees the males are called drones.

As with most social insects the ant society is made up of castes: a caste is a group of ants that is physically distinguished and represents a division of labour – e.g. queen ants are one caste (they lay eggs), the workers another (they forage or carry out nest duties), but males are not strictly a caste because they are of a different sex. In most species of ants, when mating takes place, males and queens have membranous wings which are later lost. The queens and males are usually quite physically distinct, not only are the queens bigger but they differ in shape also. Queen ants sometimes have a humped thorax . Where the different castes and sub-castes look different, being specially adapted to carry out their specific tasks, the species is said to be polym orphic. True workers are wingless, and the worker caste may include subcastes – minor workers, medium workers or large workers (soldiers). The proportion of sub-castes in a population of ants may be genetically determined. For example with *Pheidole dentata* the majors represent 5–15% of the total worker force and this ratio is always maintained; if in a laboratory colony most of the major workers are experimentally removed, more majors are produced. The environment may influence the caste ratio to a certain degree: when a colony is starved the ratio of majors to minors increases because larger majors are able to go without food longer than minors. In fire ants (*Solenopsis invicta*) majors are more common during late winter and spring because they are more tolerant of harsh conditions than smaller workers.

The worker caste

Minor workers, medium workers and major workers can be recognised by their size differences and the fact that certain parts of the body, like the head and jaws, may have grown out of proportion to the rest. Major workers usually include soldier ants but in some species there may be a separate soldier caste as well. In the fire ant (*Solenopsis geminata*) the medium and major workers have huge heads and blunt mandibles adapted for crushing

Queen ant

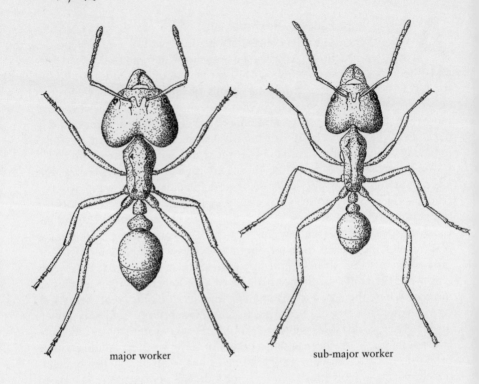

major worker

sub-major worker

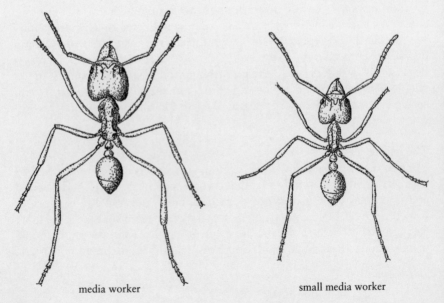

media worker

small media worker

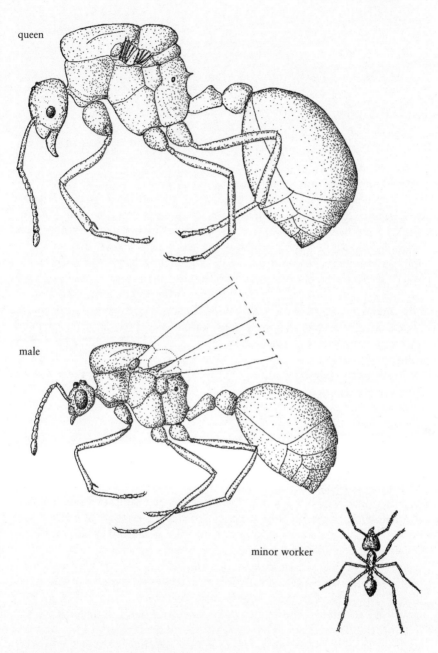

queen

male

minor worker

Polymorphic leaf-cutting ants (Atta)

I'M A LAUNDRY WORKER

seeds. The worker ants of the marauder species(*Pheidologeton diversus*), which live in S.E. Asia, have a head width more than 2.5mm, about ten times that of ordinary foraging workers of the same species, their main duty being to remove large objects in the pathway of foragers. Another good example of a species with polymorphic workers is leaf-cutting ants (*Atta* and *Acromyrmex*). Leaf-cutting ants cultivate a fungus inside their nest which is grown to feed the queen and her brood. The fungus grows on bits of leaves cut and brought into the nest by foraging workers. The minor workers are tiny and are responsible for maintaining the fungus garden in a healthy state by removing alien fungal spores, transplanting pieces of the garden and adding fresh leaf material. These workers are small enough to get deep into the soft spongy layers of the garden. The medium workers prepare the leaves by chewing them when they are brought into the nest by the foraging workers who cut the leaves from plants outside. Foraging workers vary in size, the largest of them being major workers. There is a separate soldier caste, which is larger still, and which spends most of the day doing very little but springs into action when danger threatens the colony. The minor workers make up between 60–70% of the population, medium workers 30%, major workers 1–2% and the soldiers less than 1%.

Some species of ants show weak polymorphism so that only the queens are distinctly different from workers. Wood ants are an example of a weakly polymorphic species; although the workers exhibit a great variation in size (3.5–8.5mm in body length) they are not very polymorphic because they do not possess genuine structural differences to deal with the various tasks they carry out. In a species of wood ant living in Japan (*Formica yessensis*), the workers show a relationship between size and the kind of task they do. The small workers tend to carry out jobs inside the nest and collect honey-dew from aphids while the larger ones search for prey. Those workers involved with nest building are of an intermediate size between the nurse workers and the foragers. However, workers are still very flexible regarding the tasks they carry out as 4% of large workers perform brood care related tasks and 2–3% of small workers forage.

Just to make things even more complicated, many species of ants, including advanced species (Formicinae), have intermediate forms which are structurally like queens but function like workers (scientifically known as **egatogynes**). In the bull ants (*Myrmecia*) those members of the society that are part queen/worker have a tendency to go outside the nest to forage for food.

To vary the usual set-up, in primitive ponerine ants the queens are replaced by workers who lay eggs and gather food, whereas in some social parasitic ants the workers are redundant and the society consists of only queens.

Males generally do not carry out any duties (apart from sex) and have short lives. However, male carpenter ants (*Camponotus*) appear to be an exception to the rule as some males have been observed to feed other ants and remain in the nest overwinter (usually the males do not survive the winter). True polymorphism is generally confined to female ants, the queen being one caste and workers another.

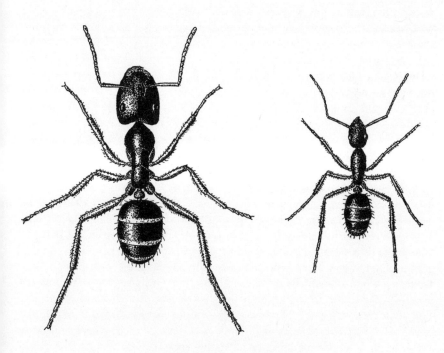

Major and minor carpenter ants

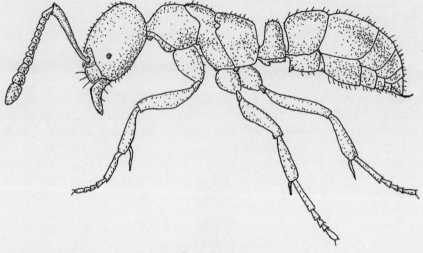

Ponerine ant

A mid-life crisis

As workers age a number of physiological changes take place inside them. In some species the workers are born with ovaries and may be capable of laying eggs, but as the workers age their ovaries degenerate and the workers themselves change their behaviour. These changes are probably caused by changes in hormones, and will affect the tasks the workers perform. Generally, workers progress from duties inside the nest, such as feeding and caring for the ant larvae, to searching for food outside the nest. This is universal among ants, bees and wasps except very primitive species: in the ant *Amblypone pallipes* there is no division of labour based on age, both young and old care for the brood.

It is not a rigid system – there may be an overlap of age groups doing a specific job, or two or three age groups may do several jobs. Young workers that remain inside the nest, often referred to as 'nurse workers', gradually venture nearer to the nest entrances and, as they get older, seem to pluck up the courage to go outside. They now become foragers and are close to the end of their life span. The foragers take all the risks; foraging is a very hazardous business and workers often come to grief during foraging trips through battles with rival ants colonies, predators or accidents. Wood ant workers may live for up to three years in a nest in the laboratory but under natural conditions it is difficult to tell. In harvester ants (*Pogonomyrmex owyheei*) the workers live for an average of two weeks. It has been shown by scientific studies that only 16% of the workers forage outside at any time, the remainder of the worker force are 'locked up' as reserves. The foragers have been known as the 'disposable caste' because they are the old.

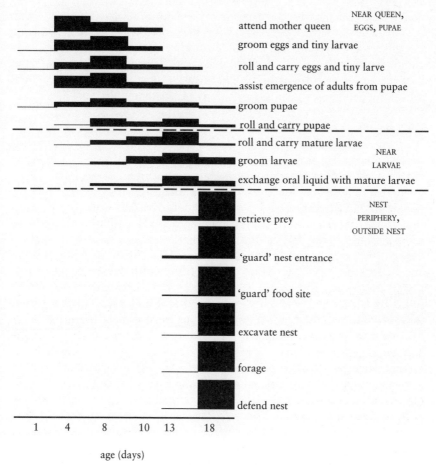

*The division of labour of worker ants (*Pheidole dentata) *and the change of their duties with age. As the workers grow older they shift from working at the centre of the nest to foraging outside. The sum of the frequencies in each histogram is 1.(After Hölldobler and Wilson, 1990)*

For queen and colony?

Altruistic behaviour in ants has been well documented in scientific literature; ants are ready to forfeit their lives for the survival of their colony. However, the apparent willingness of workers to die for the well-being of their colony has been explained by the 'selfish gene' theory. Simply, this means that living organisms contain genetic material that will stop at nothing to ensure that the genes or genetic material survive by being passed onto the next generation. Charles Darwin's theory of natural selection stipulates that the environment selects the most favourable genes, which are then passed to the offspring. Darwin could not understand, at first, how natural selection could work in social insects, since workers are normally sterile so could not pass successful genes to offspring. The answer is that in social insects natural selection operates at the family or colony rather than individual level.

Kin selection

If a gene exists for altruistic behaviour then it will be passed from the queen to her offspring. The workers will ensure that the gene survives in the population by protecting their sisters and brothers at the cost of their own lives. The theory of kin selection is that workers are more closely related to their sister workers than they would be to their own offspring (if they could have offspring) because ants share all the genetic material of the same father but only half that of the mother: the father has only one set of chromosomes, as males are produced from unfertilised eggs (see p. 33), and queens have two sets since they are born of fertilised eggs. So it is better for workers to invest in sterile sister workers which enables ants to function as social insects. However, the theory collapses because queens may mate more than once, with different males; also, the existence of colonies with more than one queen (polygynous) violates the theory of kin selection as some workers will be unrelated since they come from different fathers. Therefore an alternative theory has been put forward that the queens are parasites on the workers, and the workers are enslaved to care for the queen and her brood. Since workers are sterile it is in their best interests to stick around as the production of sisters is the only means they have of passing on their inheritance by enhancing the survival and reproductive capability of the colony as a whole. Queens can control the sex ratio by the type of eggs they lay (fertilised or unfertilised eggs) but worker control may be achieved by the quality of food they feed to the larvae – poor food will prevent queens from being produced.

A more plausible theory is that the queens and workers live together in a kind of mutual relationship. Each individual acts for its own benefit using the benefits of group living (e.g. protection against predators or kinship) which indirectly becomes an advantage to the colony as a whole.

The number of queens that live in an ants' nest depends on the species and the method of founding a new colony (p.41). Many species have one queen in each nest, e.g. black garden ants (*Lasius niger*), leaf-cutting ants and most types of wood ants. Those nests that have only one queen are called 'monogynous colonies'. Generally wood ants or red garden ants (*Myrmica* sp.) have many queens, even hundreds per nest – known as 'polygynous colonies'. It is interesting that some polygynous wood ant colonies only produce males in the spring (workers later on) and no virgin queens. This possibly reduces competition for males between virgin queens which are born in other wood ant nests close by.

Most polygynous colonies of wood ants invest in at least 50% males, because workers may no longer be sisters. In monogynous colonies more females are produced than males.

Recognition of kin
If ant colonies are to benefit, in the long term, from the altruistic behaviour of their sisters, they must be able to recognise their own kin. Kin or nest mate recognition is achieved by odour; ants from different colonies, even of the same species, smell differently. The odour of ants is due to a blend of substances, chiefly long chains of hydrocarbons, secreted from glands located in the head and thorax. The unique blend of chemicals gives each ant a kind of 'membership card' to say it belongs to that particular colony. A worker encountering other workers of a different colony (even of the same species) with the wrong 'membership card' is in danger of being dismembered.

The scent of newly hatched workers is learned by the rest of the colony and it is likely that some of the queen's recognition chemicals are transferred to larvae and young workers. It has been discovered that wood ant nurse workers immediately after they have hatched from the pupae learn to recognise young ants of their own nest. The first fifteen days after they hatch is crucial, for it is during this period that they get to know the chemical signal associated with their own cocoons. In the laboratory, nurse workers that are not exposed to cocoons during this period of their lives will eat any cocoons that they come into contact with, even cocoons of their own species. On the other hand, if wood ant workers are presented with cocoons of another species during this sensitive period they will accept them as their own; for example *Formica rufa* will rear the cocoons of *Formica lugubris* if these are the cocoons they came into contact with during the sensitive period. The larvae and cocoons are almost certainly impregnated with a chemical substance which enables workers to recognise brood as their own.

Obviously, scent plays an important role in an ant society. Ants that are isolated from their colony for 4 or 5 weeks may acquire a different scent. If these ants are returned to their original colony they may not be recognised by fellow workers and killed. It is likely that ants incorporate into their recognition system different odours from diet and their surroundings.

The recognition chemical comes mainly from the ant's head and is spread over the rest of the ant's body by grooming or contact with nest mates.

Scientific studies on several species of ants has revealed that the chemical signals associated with nest mate recognition are highly volatile. Dead ants do not produce the right chemical signal, so dead workers are carried to the refuse pile.

Communication

Ants communicate by chemical signals (pheromones), so their sense of smell is highly developed; the cells that detect smells are located in the antennae and mouthparts. There are at least 11 glands from which pheromones may be produced. The poison gland produces various substances, not all necessarily venoms, some of which are used in communication; one of these is a chemical: methyl-4-methylpyrrole-2-carboxylate. Depending on the amount released different behavioural responses occur: at low concentrations workers use the substance to find their way and at higher concentrations it is used to attract other workers.

Pheromones may be a mixture of different chemicals, often from different glands. Red ants (*Myrmica*) secrete undecane from the Dufour's gland to mark territory, but when making a trail between food and the nest, substances from the poison glands are added. The proportions in which the substances are mixed make them species specific so that the trail laid down by one species may be avoided by another.

It is interesting that the substances produced by various glands are in fact by-products of metabolism which have, through evolution, been put to good use. Many species of ants of the Dolichoderinae and Formicinae have lost the ability to sting but still retain the poison sac and venom, the venom being used in communication instead of defence. Effective chemical communication and weaponry is a far superior line of defence rather than stinging, hence advanced species have lost this ability. The fact that many of these chemicals are volatile makes them ideal for making a trails to food, though the trail has to be reinforced by the constant passage of ants along it otherwise it just evaporates away.

Pheromones are used to raise the alarm in emergency situations and substances produced by the mandibular glands can induce ants to become more aggressive. The African weaver ant (*Oecophylla longinoda*) illustrates how a series of chemicals can be put together to convey a message that results in an action. The weaver ant workers produce a series of pheromone substances from their mandibular glands. First, a highly volatile substance alerts other workers to danger; then a less volatile chemical orientates them towards the source of trouble and finally a non-volatile chemical, which is deposited on the hostile source (a possible predator), causes them to bite it.

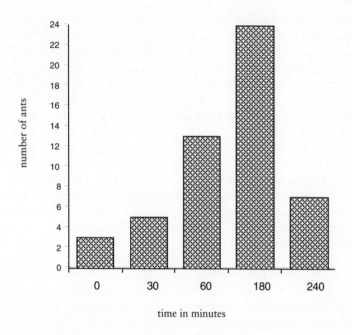

The recruitment of black garden ants to a drop of honey (0.5 ml). The histogram illustrates the rate at which worker ants arrive at a food source. The number of ants feeding on the honey were counted at 30 minute intervals. At 240 minutes the honey was almost gone so there were fewer ants.

Mass recruitment

Ants are extremely well organised when it comes to food that is too large for an individual to bring back alone. An individual worker in this situation will alert or 'recruit' other workers from the nest to the food. The finder or scout ant returns to the nest, laying a pheromone trail as it goes. This trail leads nest mates to the food. However, once inside the nest the scout must convince its fellow workers that the food source is worth while. The release of a pheromone is usually enough. Harvester ant (*Pogonomyrmex*) scouts on return lower their abdomens and extrude the sting which is dragged along the ground. The contents of the sting poison gland alert nest mates and they soon pick up the trail laid by the scout. Many ants reinforce the presence of food by performing strange movements to excite fellow workers into following a scent trail. The movements are called a 'motor display' and may involve vibrating the antennae, regurgitation of food to other workers or thrusting the head into the face of another worker. A motor display by a worker gets its nest mates highly excited, and the excitement travels through the worker population like a shock wave. Once a population of foraging workers has been alerted it does not take them long to pick up the scent trail. At the food source more and more workers arrive as the numbers of ants returning to the nest with information about the food increases.

Ants running tandem

Tandem running may be a primitive method used by some ants to recruit fellow workers. When a scout has returned to the nest, and performed its display to the other workers, soon one worker will touch the abdomen of the scout and the tandem run begins with the scout leading and the alerted worker following closely behind touching the leader's gaster or hind legs with its antennae. Should the contact be broken then the leading ant extrudes its sting and releases a calling pheromone until contact is resumed. As only one ant is recruited at any time, tandem running is considered primitive in comparison to 'mass recruitment'. Tandem running is used by species of ponerine ants in response to food and may be used by other species to recruit to new nest sites; some species of carpenter ants do this.

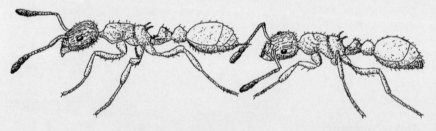

Tandem running in a pair of workers

Recruitment to a new home

Ants may move house because of various changes in the environment in the vicinity of the nest, for example, the overshadowing of the nest by vegetation making the area too cool or damp. In red garden ants the search for a new home is begun by scouts, who explore the area for a new nest site. When a suitable site is found, the scouts return to the old nest to recruit further workers. A returning scout extrudes its sting, touching the ground, laying a pheromone trail to lead the way back to the chosen nest site. The recruits follow the leader very closely in single file. Again, the leading scout extrudes its sting, releasing a pheromone to attract followers. Soon there is a mass emigration from the old nest. Pupae, larvae and young workers are all carried to the new nest, the workers doing the transporting also releasing pheromones from their poison glands to reinforce the trail. The queens usually follow on foot. Some workers then return to the old nest, for a final check, to make sure nobody has been left behind. The scouts never go very far from the old nest, but the move will probably take all day.

USE OF SOUND

As well as using scents, ants are able to communicate by using sound. Leaf–cutting worker ants are known to produce sound by scraping a kind of scraper along a file located on two abdominal segments. The sound is produced when the ants raise and lower their abdomens. The mechanism is called 'stridulation' (the same as grasshoppers) and is used to alert nest mates of danger. The sound is not transmitted through the air but by vibration through the ground. When a leaf-cutting ant nest collapses the buried occupants stridulate to alert nest mates who are able to dig their way in.

It is possible that stridulation is a means by which leaf-cutting ants communicate the presence of a source of leaves suitable for cutting to be used in the fungus garden. The mechanism was discovered by using scientific equipment sensitive to vibration. As the worker ants cut the leaves, with their jaws, they stridulate and the vibration alerts nest mates to the cutting site. Leaf-cutting ants are very fussy about the leaves that they select, cutting only those that are palatable and have high nutrient content for growth of the fungus garden. Stridulation may communicate the quality of the leaves that are being cut.

Making more ants

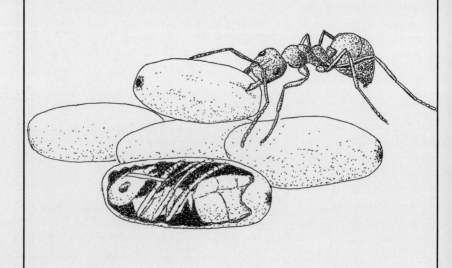

A colony of ants grows without any sexual reproduction – apart from the intial mating of the mother queen – taking place. The workers are produced from eggs laid by the queen. She is basically a store of eggs, which are fertilised by the sperm she has stored from previous mating. When the colony is mature it stops producing more workers and starts to reproduce itself sexually by producing winged ants. These are the reproductive ants: males and virgin queens. The production of reproductive ants is very expensive for the nest in terms of energy input as they do nothing to aid the growth of the colony, but will eventually fly away to found another colony. The male ants serve no purpose in the ant society other than to copulate with virgin queens. Therefore, it is important that the colony is established with a large enough worker population to bring in plenty of food to supply energy for the queen and the larvae, which develop into winged ants during the spring.

Ant development

Queens and workers come from fertilised eggs, but male ants actually develop from unfertilised eggs; how the queen manages to lay eggs which are not fertilised, since she has large quantities of sperm stored in her body, is a mystery. One answer is that in temperate species the eggs start to mature, in the ovary, around late winter and are not fertilised because the temperature inside the nest is too low to allow sperm to penetrate the eggs. If wood ant queens are kept below 15°C they deposit eggs which produce winged males, above 15°C the eggs develop into young queens or workers. However, this does not answer the question why ants of warmer climates are able to produce males from unfertilised eggs; presumably the queen must exert some physiological or chemical control to prevent the sperm fertilising the eggs. Time taken for eggs to hatch varies with species, but wood ant eggs hatch in about two weeks.

In many species, worker ants are capable of laying eggs which, because they cannot be fertilised, always develop into males. In colonies where the queen is dead it may not be possible to replace her so the whole nest will eventually die. As a last resort the workers lay eggs which produce male ants. These males can fly away and mate with virgin queens from a different nest; if the young mated queen is successful at founding a new nest, some of the genes from the doomed nest will be inherited by her offspring. Under normal circumstances workers are inhibited, by chemical messages, from laying eggs if a queen is present. However, in some species the workers will still lay eggs even if the queen is in residence, but such eggs are never allowed to develop – they are used to feed the developing brood.

Weaver ant workers are exceptional in being able to lay eggs which de-

Wood ant and cocoons

velop into virgin queens or workers, as well as males, without fertilisation by a process called 'parthenogenesis', which is common in the insect world: for example aphids can reproduce in this way. In the first instance the queen seems to be superfluous but she is still required for sexual reproduction to incorporate fresh genetic material into the ant population. The workers are only able to lay eggs in parts of the nest where the queen is absent.

The creature that emerges from an ant's egg looks nothing like an ant! Like most insects, ants must go through a series of developmental stages before they start to resemble the adult. What crawls out from an ant's eggs is a tiny grub called a larva (plural: larvae). The ant larva has a mouth at one end and an anus at the other and is covered by a delicate skin or cuticle. At this stage the ant larvae spend all their time feeding. As they grow they start to moult; their outer skin begins to split open to reveal a new skin which has already formed beneath. This is the second stage of growth; although it looks similar to the first, it will be bigger. From the cuticle project numerous little hair–like structures which protect the larvae from rough handling by the workers as they move them from place to place in the nest; the hairs also enable the larvae to stick together so they can be moved in one go. Ant larvae will shed their skins three or four times, then they cease feeding and expel their body wastes before the final stage of their development cycle.

The final stage is the pupa (plural: pupae). The pupa develops beneath

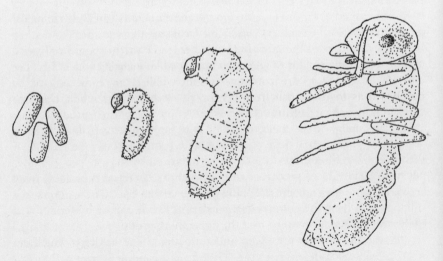

Developmental stages of an ant (egg, larvae, pupae)

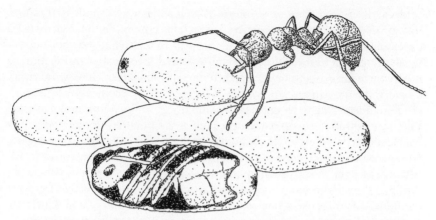

Cocoons of wood ants with one cocoon cut away to reveal the pupa inside

the larval skin and looks very much like the adult folded up. When the pupal skin begins to tear the rest of it will be peeled away by the workers to help the young adult to escape. The change from the larval stage to the adult is known as metamorphosis, and lasts for three to four weeks. Young ants are called 'callows'. They are very pale in colour and to begin with have great difficulty in walking. They remain inside the nest for several weeks, cared for by the nurse workers until their cuticles harden and darken: again, this takes three or four weeks.

In ant species of the Formicinae group, which includes the wood ants, the pupae are enclosed in silk cocoons. The final stage larvae spin the cocoon from silk produced in the salivary glands, attaching themselves to soil particles or something similar to get a foothold while they spin the cocoon. The cocoons of wood ants are sometimes wrongly called 'ant eggs' and can be purchased as food for fish from certain pet stores. Incidentally, the little black dot at one end of the cocoon is the point where the larvae ejects its waste after spinning the cocoon.

Caste determination
The differentiation of the larvae into different types of workers is dictated by social and environmental conditions inside the nest. For example the number of soldiers in a colony of *Pheidole* ants is maintained at about 5% of the worker population in the nest, so if the number of soldiers gets too high few larvae develop into soldiers and *vice versa*. The soldiers produce a pheromone which desensitises the larvae to a hormone known as Juvenile hormone, in their blood, which would normally cause them to mature into

soldiers. It appears that in response to environmental signals or requirements of the colony, developing larvae, up to a critical stage in their development, may be switched from one type of worker to another.

Development of the larvae into young queens is controlled by the mother queen through a pheromone which influences how the workers treat the larvae in the nest. In red garden ants if the queen is to prevent the formation of virgin queens she must physically maintain contact with her worker force to ensure that the pheromone reaches the entire population of nurse workers. The workers, under the influence of the queen's pheromone, feed the larvae a poor watery diet and behave in an aggressive manner towards them. In the final stage the larvae are bitten so hard them that they may be scared. This rough treatment not surprisingly speeds up their rate of development and causes them grow into workers. (Is there a lesson for us human parents in this?) In the summer the queens lose control, probably because they produce less pheromone, and lay large eggs that are allowed to become young queens. A high ratio of workers to larvae may also result in young queens being reared. The reason for this may be that the more workers there are in a nest the less likely they are to be exposed to the queen's pheromone, so these workers rear virgin queens.

Temperature and day length are thought to be the principal factors controlling the production of queen biased larvae during late summer; these larvae are destined to hatch into queens, but the way they are treated by workers can override this so that they will develop into workers; also aging queens lay fewer eggs, which are larger and queen biased. Larger eggs means larger larvae and the workers feed them a rich protein diet which makes them grow bigger and prevents them changing into workers. By autumn they have reached the pupal stage and hibernate over the winter until the following spring ready for their nuptial flight. The winter chilling is an im-

Larvae of myrmicine ant

portant factor which enables the larvae to develop into virgin queens.

Others species have similar mechanisms to control queen production; usually the presence of an egg-laying queen is enough to prevent new queens from being born. In polygynous nests the queens are usually absent from the part of the nest where young queens are reared. In spring wood ant queens come to the surface of the nest to lay queen biased eggs, afterwards moving back down to lay worker biased eggs. Young wood ant queens and males develop in complete isolation from the mother queens in the nest. They are cared for by the workers in a separate chamber in the nest. Under certain conditions the development of queen biased eggs can be reversed and the larvae grow into workers instead. In some ants this can occur during the third stage larvae moult, but in wood ants the queen biased eggs can still become workers, providing no more than 72 hours has passed after hatching; eggs predisposed to become winged (queen) ants will do so if they are fed high quality food within 72 hours of hatching, if not they become workers.

ANT RHYTHMS

Ants do not sleep but they do have periods when they rest. Rest periods alternate with periods of activity, and the busy periods continue throughout our twenty-four-hour day. Video recordings made of ants inside nest boxes, housed in the laboratory, have shown that the activity of individual ants is highly synchronised with each other showing pulses of activity every 15 or 30 minutes. In fact, whole colonies of ants exhibit rhythmical changes in their level of activity so that they become active all at the same time. Individual ants which are placed on their own still have bursts of activity followed by rest but the periods of activity are not rhythmical. A rhythm is only induced when ants are in a group.

Nuptial flight

Before mating, most species of ant embark on a marriage flight, something they will only do once in their lives: the virgin queens spend the rest of their lives laying eggs, and the males die. This ritual is important because it promotes outbreeding by increasing the prospects that males and young queens, living miles from each other, will come into contact and mate. Outbreeding populations may acquire vigorous genes which produce new types of individuals, which is important if a species is to survive in an unstable or continually changing environment. If a species survives its genes will be passed onto the next generation. This is the fundamental mechanism of evolution: the population most suited to the environment has the best chance of survival.

Ants show seasonality in flight times. In Britain wood ants take to the air in late May and June. The black backed meadow ant (*Formica pratensis*) has a second mating flight in September, when a second batch of eggs, laid in July, develop into winged ants. Winged forms of the black garden ant (*Lasius niger*) can be observed scurrying across the pavements, in towns and cities, around late July and August. Black garden ants leave their nests, en masse, in the late afternoon. They fly quite high using air currents to lift them; pairing may take place on the wing, as the males are much smaller than the queens and the queens are able to carry them. Ants that inhabit tropical or desert conditions wait until the rainy season before they fly. For example, harvester ants (*Pogonomyrmex*) in Arizona fly on the warm sunny days that follow heavy rain.

Ants will only fly if the air temperature and humidity outside the nest are ideal. Winged ants may assemble, daily, close to the entrances of the nest, but if the weather is not right they stay put. In fact, carpenter ant (*Camponotus herculeanus*) workers may hold the winged ants back to prevent them from taking off when conditions are poor, only to drag them out again when the weather improves!

When the conditions are right queens and males swarm from the nests at the same time. Their flight times are synchronised by an internal body clock. Similar species which share the same habitat may fly at different times of the day. A good example is, again, the harvester ants of Arizona where four different species have different flight times: 10.00–11.30; 11.00–13.00; 15.30–

17.00; and 16.30–18.00. This is probably a mechanism to prevent similar species from hybridising. However, hybrid species do occur amongst ants, particularly wood ants where colonies of closely related species might come into contact and mate successfully; the offspring share external characteristics of both species, making their identification an entomologist's nightmare! The closer the species are genetically, the more likely the hybrid is to be fertile: different species of wood ants are very much alike genetically.

Some ants, like red garden ants (*Myrmica*), choose a particular location where both sexes congregate and mate. They return to the same site every year; consequently hundreds of winged ants are sometimes seen swarming around tree tops, buildings, rock outcrops or even mountain tops. Winged wood ants, living in the Swiss Jura mountains, are known to fly a short distance for a rendezvous in a meadow for a winged orgy.

It takes an enormous amount of energy for ants to fly. This energy is obtained from stored carbohydrate, in the form of glycogen. The ability of ants to fly varies with different species, some are poor flyers or don't fly at all. Scientific studies have shown that non-flyers have very low levels of glycogen; this may be related to the fact that they mature very quickly, which does not allow time for the glycogen stores to build up. It seems that British wood ants generally lack the power of good flight. They may fly no more than 2 metres (6 feet) from the nest; pairing takes place on the ground or on vegetation close to the nest. In most wood ant colonies the winged ants do not bother to fly all, but depart on foot and mate on the ground or on the surface of the nest. However, in the Swiss Jura mountains the flights of wood ants are longer. The males look for females by flying about 50 centimetres (20 inches) above the ground, lured to the females by scent or pheromone (see below). Each wood ant female is soon surrounded by several males seeking her adoration. In the Argentine ant (*Iridomyrmex humilis*) the young queens never fly and mating takes place inside the nest. In some desert species only the males take to the air. They fly to different nests and mate with the females inside. The South American army ants have queens which are wingless; the males have wings and fly in the evening searching for virgin queens.

Mating
Depending on the species, young queens do mate more than once and with different males. The queens have only have one maiden flight so they make the most of it. After copulation a queen acquires enough sperm to last her a lifetime. During copulation the abdomens of the male and female are joined at the tip. The male then passes sperm into a sperm storage sack in the female. This sack is directly connected to the ovary-duct. As the eggs travel down the ovary-duct, from the ovary, they are fertilised inside the queen.

The sperm is stored in the queen until she dies – which may be a long time, queens of wood ants and leaf-cutters can live up to 20 years!

Seductive scents

Many ants employ volatile chemical substances or pheromones to 'call' the opposite sex. Female wood ants living in the Swiss Jura mountains release a seductive scent, from the Dufour's gland in the gaster, to lure the males. The scent has been extracted from the gland in the laboratory and was found to be a substance known as undecane. Undecane is the universal medium for ants: the basis for a multitude of behavioural actions. One version of its chemical structure turns it into an aphrodisiac to drive males wild with sexual desire; another variation, released by carpenter ant males from special glands in the head (mandibular glands), causes females to swarm. Even humans can smell this aroma, though the effects on them are not as dramatic. Once the females are on the wing they are pursued by hopeful males. Volatile chemicals produced from the mandibular glands of male leaf-cutter ants increase the excitability of workers around the time of the nuptial flight; the workers become very aggressive and attack any object in their path. This probably protects the winged ants from predators just before take off.

In Britain, large swarms of a tiny ant (*Leptothorax acervorum*) have been observed on mountain tops alighting on the stems of grass and other vertical structures. The female then sets about 'calling' to the males by releasing a pheromone. A 'calling' female is noticeable because she adopts a typical posture of head down and gaster up. The sting protrudes and it is likely that a volatile chemical is released from the poison sack. As the substance diffuses through the air the female is soon surrounded by males in a ratio of about 1:10!

Primitive female ants depend totally on pheromones to advertise their willingness to mate. One Australian ponerine (*Rhytidoponera metallica*) has no queens as such; the females are wingless and behave as workers. The females come to the nest entrances and adopt a calling posture: the head and thorax are pressed on the ground while the gaster is raised and bowed, the females then proceed to 'call' the males by releasing a pheromone from glands in the gaster. The males are winged and fly from other nests, attracted to the females by their alluring scent.

A queen's right to say no!

Male ants can be very persistent when it comes to sex – after all it is their only function in life! So a queen has to say no at some point. Harvester ant queens will stridulate, to produce a sound, when they no longer want to mate. A queen who has copulated with several males will have a plentiful supply of sperm. She produces a series of short chirps to signify that she is no longer game for approaching males. This for some reason puts the male off. The sound is made by rubbing a scraper and a file located on the 3rd and 4th abdominal segments, as the abdomen bends upwards and then downward. The sound lasts for approximately 200 milliseconds with an energy of 1–9 kilo hertz, which is audible to the human ear.

Fate of winged ants

For male ants it is the end of the road; after serving their purpose they die. Male wood ants that live in the forests of Tien-Shan mountains, in Russia, have a rather horrible death: the sexual behaviour of this wood ant is unusual because while they are copulating the female bites off the male's abdomen. The male then flies away, minus his rear end; he may survive two of three days in this condition before he gives up the ghost.

After mating, the chances of survival for young queens are reduced; they must set about founding a new nest, which is a risky business. Some species may do this task alone or co-operate with several other young queens in building a new nest. Young queens left outside are likely to become a tasty snack for predators. Out of a thousand or so leaf-cutter queens that swarm from a single nest only 2–3 may be successful in founding new colonies.

Colony founding by queens

How a young queen sets about finding a new home in which to bring up her family varies a great deal in different species of ants. Mated queens that enter polygynous colonies have a better chance of producing brood in these nests because a worker force is already established. Even so there is a risk that she might be killed by the workers. One possible reason for this is that there is an element of 'selfishness' among workers who prefer their sister queens, to whom they are more closely related. A young queen who has come from another colony would produce workers which would, in theory, decrease the level of kinship within that colony. What's interesting is that a queen from another colony that has not flown or mated is readily accepted! A possible reason behind this is that a virgin queen will produce only males (from unfertilised eggs), these males fly away and thus do not affect kinship.

Claustral cell

Some ants allow only one queen to reside in the nest. In these monogynous colonies, the young queen must found the nest without help. In black garden ants, after mating, the queen removes her wings and looks for a suitable site to begin her nest. The choice of nest site is very important as it must be in a good position where it will attain a high enough temperature for the brood to develop. If there is too much shade it could get too cold. When the queen is happy with the nest site she digs into soft soil making a small chamber and seals herself in – the claustral cell. The young queen has no food or worker force and obtains nourishment from her wing muscles, which by now have started to liquefy and are gradually absorbed back into her body. The queen will remain in her cell over the winter and in the following spring she lays her first batch of eggs. These eggs become the first generation of worker ants. The first workers are very small and when old enough they leave the claustral cell to look for food outside. Meanwhile the queen continues to lay eggs, some of which are fed to the developing larvae. Only 10–20% of the eggs hatch, the rest are eaten.

Leaf-cutting ant queens bring their own food supply with them when founding a nest. The queen leaf-cutting ant brings with her a small piece of fungus, which she carries in a little pouch inside her mouth, from the natal nest. Her wing muscles provide her with energy until the first workers hatch. When the workers are fully grown they go out to procure cut leaves, which are then used to cultivate a new fungus garden; the fungus is used to feed the ant larvae (p. 47).

In primitive species, such as the Ponerinae or Australian bull ants, the founding queen leaves the claustral cell to forage for insects and plant juices on which to feed her young. There is an element of risk involved here because if she is killed the colony perishes. When the first generation of workers are old enough to forage the bull ant queen seals herself inside the nest chamber and continues to lay more eggs.

Queen co-operation

In some ants a group of queens may set up house together, even though the species is generally monogynous. Co-founding of a new nest makes the task easier. In fire ants dominant queens remain inside the nest while subordinate queens go outside to collect food and protect the nest. The dominant queens stay inside to take care of and feed the brood of the other queens as well as their own. In the end only one queen will survive as rival queens fight to the death once the brood matures. Although only one queen will live, the dead queens have contributed some of their genetic material to a new generation of ants through their brood. Co-founding also has an advantage over claustral founded nests in that many nests with only one queen perish or are destroyed by other ants; queen co-operation benefits from the 'safety in numbers' principle.

Temporary social parasitism

Some queen ants invade the nest of another species (the host), murder the host queen and fool the workers into raising their brood. Under these circumstances the queen is said to be a temporary parasite because once the workers develop they gradually take over the colony as the host workers die out. A wood ant queen can trick the workers of another species, *Formica fusca*, into accepting her into their nest. How the wood ant queen manages to be so devious is not known for sure but it has been reported that she plays dead and the *fusca* workers carry her in as prey. Once inside she decapitates the *fusca* queen and acquires her scent by licking and biting the headless corpse. She now smells like the *fusca* queen and is hailed the new queen of the colony! The tyrant queen then lays her eggs and the larvae are raised and nourished by the *fusca* workers. The colony eventually becomes a wood ant colony when the *fusca* workers are all dead.

Nest splitting

Ants are able to increase their population and number of nests without involving sex. This is the most common method of reproduction in the wood ants: you will remember that these are polygynous ants, with many queens in one nest. The population of one large nest may divide because of overcrowding or lack of food. The split is initiated by the workers which build a new nest elsewhere and carry some of the fertile queens and brood to the new site. Once settled into her new home the queen will then continue to lay eggs which finally develop into young worker ants: thus the population will grow. It is often noted, in wood ants, that smaller nests are 'budded off' from a large nest in this way. This often results in the large nest being surrounded by several tiny nests. In the Swiss Jura this has led to large wood ant colonies, known as 'super colonies', where all the nests appear to be interconnected with pathways. 'Super colonies' in the Swiss Jura comprise around 1,200 nests in 172 acres (70 ha) acres of habitat.

What ants eat and how they get their food

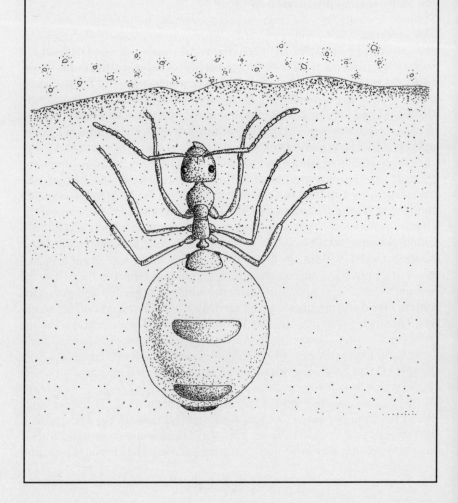

Ants eat a variety of plant and animal food, including decaying matter and secretions from plants or insects. Animals may even, in the case of African army ants, include small vertebrates such as lizards and snakes. Some species even go as far as to grow their own food in the form of a fungus garden or 'farm' insects for their sweet sugar secretions.

The means by which ants find food varies among different species. Foraging ants may employ a scout who will go forth, find a food source and recruit others to the food by means of a scent trail. Primitive ants may forage alone but advanced species co-operate in bringing prey back to the nest.

An army marches on its stomach

Imagine a vast army of hunters moving overland with military precision, and you have a good impression of the army ants. Totally blind (although they are sensitive to light; and, interestingly, the males retain their power of sight), they organise themselves into a column or swarm of marauding ants using the most intricate means of chemical communication. The nest of the army ants is called a 'bivouac', a temporary nest made by the workers hooking themselves to branches and then the rest of the colony attaching itself to them: it consists entirely of the living bodies of the workers with the queen and brood at the centre (see p.73).

There are two major groups of army ants, the *Dorylus* from Africa and *Eciton* from Central and South America. The size of the populations of many species of army ants can be enormous, reaching one million in *Eciton* and 20 million in *Dorylus*. The life cycle of the colony involves two phases, the 'statary phase' (sedentary phase) concerned with reproduction and the 'nomadic phase' when the population becomes hungry and begins raiding food sources. During the 'statary phase' the nest or bivouac remains in the same place and only a few ants go out on small raids and return to the nest in the evening. During the 'nomadic phase' the whole nest gets up and goes. The queen, brood and ant guests are all carried along with the marauding workers. They then put up in temporary bivouacs at night. The stimulus for raiding behaviour is thought to come from the young adult workers which hatch from the pupae in the nest when more food is needed. Raids take place daily for 14–17 days before the colony settles again at the 'statary phase' of its life cycle, which lasts for about three weeks.

Two strategies are employed by the army ants in raids: either the raids are in the form of columns of ants which spread through the undergrowth like fingers or they swarm in an advancing front taking anything in their path; the column may be 65 feet (20 metres) across. The ants have powerful

Honey-pot ant

jaws which they use to bite prey, having first immobilised it by stinging. There is usually a stream of ants moving forward and another in reverse taking prey back to the nest or bivouac. It has been calculated that *Eciton burchelli* brings back approximately 100,000 prey items daily.

The army ants are notorious for killing any living animal in their path but this is a misconception, for most species raid the nests of other ants. *Eciton hamatum* feeds exclusively on ant brood. The odour of approaching *Eciton hamatum* and the rustling noise sends its victims scurrying from their nest carrying brood to the tree tops out of harm's way. Those workers that escape the army ant raids return to the nest with brood and resume normal daily life. Raiding army ants do not destroy ant colonies but keep them in check preventing the populations from expanding by removing the brood; adult ants are not eaten because they are difficult to digest (at least by other ants – chimpanzees certainly do not think so)!

Not all animals and insects are acceptable to army ants as prey. The external skeletons of many dung (scarabaeid) beetles are too tough for the ants to dismantle, army ants are repelled by the odour of termites and stingless

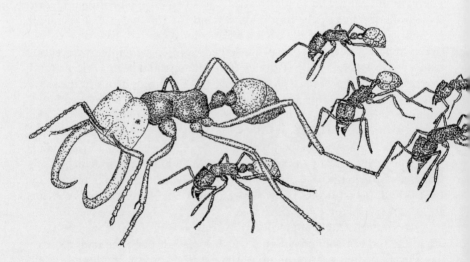

Army ants

bees will attack raiding army ants covering them with sticky propolis. They never eat the brood of other army ants even if they are of a different species.

Gardening ants

Leaf-cutting ants, also from the South and Central America, grow their own food! The ants cultivate a fungus garden in large underground chambers. The species of fungus grows nowhere else, although there are probably free-living forms that are closely related to it. The fungus has the scientific name of *Attamyces* and is related to the edible mushrooms. The ants never allow the fungus to form fruiting bodies or mushroom like structures which produce spores for reproducing, consequently the fungus is incapable of reproducing without the ants. The ants transplant bits of the fungus (fungal hyphae) to different parts of the nest and to new nest sites (see p. 42). The fungus is grown on pieces of leaves cut by the ants from trees and herbs. Other fungus growing ants which are more primitive than the leaf-cutters grow fungus on a substrate of pieces of dead insects, plant material and their own faeces.

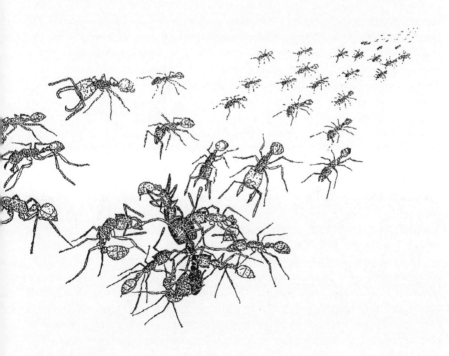

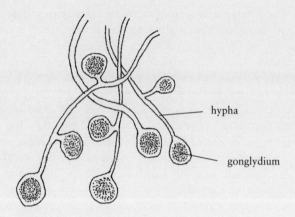

Gonglydia of leaf-cutter ant fungus

The leaf-cutting ants cut semi-circular sections from the leaves with their powerful jaws and carry the sections back to the nest. The ants will take most leaves, except poisonous ones. The leaves may also be dropped from the tree where workers at the bottom collect them and take them to the nest. Inside the nest the ants lick the leaves to remove bacteria and alien fungal spores, otherwise the garden would be overrun with other types of fungi and micro-organisms. This is a form of weeding to maintain a monoculture of *Attamyces*. It is likely that many of the secretions produced by the various glands of ants have antimicrobial properties to inhibit the growth of micro-organisms inside the nest.

Once the leaf pieces are cleaned they are cut into fragments 1–2 mm across. The fragments are then chewed to release the nutrients and planted in the fungus garden. The ants then drop some of their own anal excrement on the leaves; the excrement contains enzymes to start the digestion of leaf proteins and the tough cellulose material present in leaves. These enzymes come from the fungus itself and are not produced by the ant, the ants merely concentrate the enzymes. The fungus is eaten by the ants but it only provides about 9% of the energy required by the workers, the rest they obtain from leaf sap as they cut the leaves.

The relationship between the ants and the fungus is an example of symbiosis, which is the association of two dissimilar organisms to the mutual benefit of each. The ants bring to the fungus a continuous supply of fresh leaves and maintain the fungus in an ideal environment without competition from other micro-organisms. The ants are able to physically break down the leaf tissue and provide for the fungus a substrate into which the fungal hyphae ('stems' of the fungus) can easily penetrate; without their chewing, the wax coated layer of leaves is an effective barrier against fungal attack. The fungus benefits the ants by detoxicifying the poisonous substances present in the leaves of most plants, consequently the ants are able to exploit an enormous number of plants as a food source. The food which ants receive comes packaged in the form of gonglydia which are groups of small swellings on the fungal hyphae. The gonglydia are rich in nutrients and are fed to the queen and her brood by the workers.

LARVAL 'DOORKNOBS'

The larvae of some species of Ponerinae are peculiar in that they are covered in soft, fleshy, spine-like structures. Nobody is really sure of the function of these structures. Some of the spine-like structures may serve to protect the larvae from being eaten by their own worker ants but some species of this subfamily have two pairs of additional structures which look like 'doorknobs'. The 'doorknobs' are sticky at the tip and may serve to anchor the larvae to the ceiling or walls of the nest chamber. This would keep the larvae out of any water which may be present in the nest chamber, as these ants often nest under rotten logs of the tropical rainforest. When suspended their long slender necks, ending in powerful jaws, will be able to bend and stretch to devour any prey place near to them.

Farming ants

Many bugs (Homoptera) such as aphids produce a sweet sticky sugar secretion. This is in fact a waste product produced from the plant sap on which these insects feed and must be got rid of. To ants this substance, honey-dew, is an invaluable food source because it contains energy in the form of sugars, as well as amino acids and vitamins. The aphids live on plant stems or on plant roots in the underground chambers of ant nests. Wood ants, red ants and black garden ants milk the aphids of honey-dew and protect them from predators and aphid parasites. The ants do not physically protect the aphids but the presence and movement of the ants around aphid colonies probably deter predators from approaching the aphids. If disturbed, however, ants will pick up the aphids in the same way that they pick up their brood and carry them to safety. Many ants go as far as building little shelters for aphids around the base of plant stems from bits of vegetation. The entrances to the shelters are often too small for some aphid predators to enter hence the aphids are protected in 'cattle sheds' from enemies and harsh weather conditions.

The ants tap the hind ends of the aphids with their antennae to encourage them to produce droplets of honey-dew, which are expelled from little

Worker accepting honey-dew from an aphid

pipe-like structures on the backs of the aphids. The honey-dew is drunk by the workers and carried back to the nest in the crop; as the crop fills the gaster swells The crop may become so engorged with honey-dew that the abdomen becomes almost translucent. A set of valves closes the crop from the gut and opens when the honey is to be regurgitated. Workers regurgitate the honey-dew to other workers back at the nest by mouth to mouth contact (scientific term 'trophallaxis').

Trails of foraging wood ants may be observed ascending tree trunks leading to the aphid colonies high in the branches. Some aphids found on plant roots may have been placed there by the ants themselves. The black garden ants collect honey-dew from subterranean aphid colonies. When the aphid populations become too large the ants will eat them, which is what humans dignify with the name of culling.

Ants also collect honey-dew from different types of insects like scale insects and various bugs. Sap and resin seeping from tree bark and nectar from flowers is also favoured by many species of ants. As an example honey-dew forms 62% of the diet of wood ants while insects make up 33%, plant sap and resin from trees 4.5%, fungi and carrion 0.3% and seeds 0.2%. Honey-dew is important during early spring in temperate climates when insect prey is less abundant.

Ants that store food

Seeds are an important food source to many species of ant not only because of the nutritional value of seeds themselves but because they can be stored well. Many ants living in the most arid regions of the world are quick to exploit this by storing seeds underground. The harvesting ant *Messor pergandei* survives in Death Valley, California, by feeding on seeds stored in chambers of its nest when insect food or nectar is scarce. The workers begin foraging at dawn, collecting seeds from 14 species of plants, break off in the late morning when the sun is high, and start again in the late afternoon (when the day begins to cool) until dark. Large numbers of workers follow trunk trails and travel at least 40 metres (130 feet) from the nest; the columns of workers rotate around the nest until the whole foraging ground is covered.

The major workers act as millers and have exceptionally large heads adapted for grinding seeds with the jaws: one of the most extreme cases of this is a harvesting ant, *Acanthomyrmex*, which looks just like a head on legs. The ground seeds are then regurgitated to other workers and fed to the larvae.

In temperate areas ants may collect seed for its oil content but seeds also contain a great deal of starch. Ants will chew on the seeds; when mixed with saliva enzymes are produced from the various glands to convert starch to sugars; the mixture may then be regurgitated to nest mates as a very rich energy source.

There are species of ants whose gasters becomes so engorged with fluid that they cannot move from the nest – these ants are literally living pots of honey. The so-called honey-pot ants (*Myrmecocystus*) live in the deserts of the western United States and Mexico. The major workers become storage

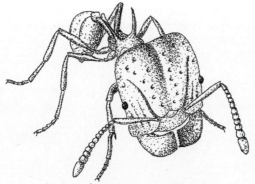

An Acanthomyrmex *major worker*

pots of sugar solution or water, supplying the entire colony with food and drink. When temperatures outside the nest are low incoming foragers fill the 'honey pots' with nectar, but when temperatures go above 30°C the 'honey pots' give up their stored liquids to the foragers.

There are many species of ant whose workers may act as food storage vessels but perhaps not in such an extreme way as *Myrmecocystus*. Young wood ant workers store energy in the fat body which is metabolised during the hibernation period to provide energy to keep the ant alive. The fat body is a clump of cells floating in the body cavity, responsible for the storage of energy in the form of fat, also glycogen and proteins (it is the creamy white substance that comes out if you stamp on a cockroach). The food stored in the crop is digested in the stomach and deposited in the abdomen as a fatty substance. This represents the energy store of an ant. Most of the food collected by the foragers is regurgitated to the young workers who store it within themselves as fat body. When the larvae hatch the following spring the fat body is mobilised and fed to the developing larvae.

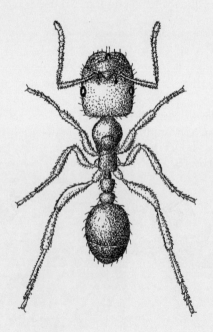

Messor barbarus, *old world harvester ant with large, pale head*

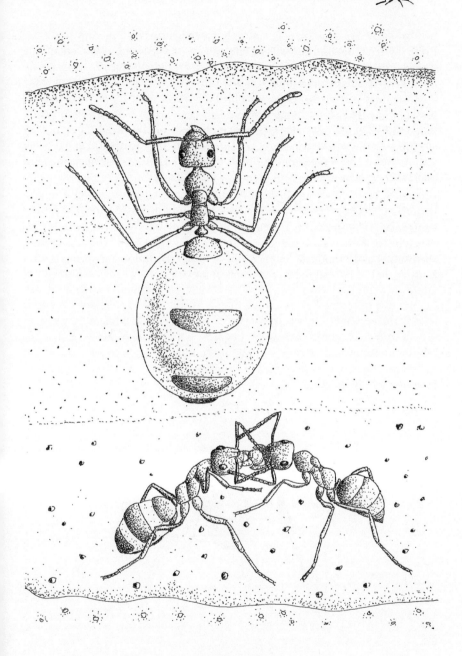

Honey-pot ants

Capturing prey

Individual workers have their own methods of capturing prey. Some ants armed with a sting may hold prey in their jaws; the ant then turns its abdomen towards the prey, to sting it. Other ants of the Ponerinae, Myrmicinae and Formicidae have trap-jaws which snap shut on the prey when contact is made (p.88). *Daceton armigerum* (Brazil) is a species that creeps up on its prey before giving chase, its jaws held at an angle of almost 180° before they snap shut on the victim. Many ants detect prey by smell, others rely on vision; wood ants have very good vision and are able to see objects move at a distance of 10 centimetres (4 inches). The workers usually grab the prey by the leg or a part of the body that the jaws can get a grip on; smooth insects like some beetles whose the legs can be withdrawn beneath the body often escape. Some ants kill their prey by injecting venom, others by stretching and pulling at it.

Foraging workers may carry small items of prey back to the nest in their jaws or drag them back backwards. Red garden ants are the tarzans of the ant world, and can drag four times their own weight; wood ants, although bigger, can only drag or lift twice theirs. Wood ants will generally attack insects the size of bluebottles or wasps. If the prey is too large more workers are recruited – it could take several of hours for a group of wood ants, all pulling in opposite directions, mind you, to move an item of prey 10 metres (32 feet). Other species, like the pharaoh ant, tear off bits of prey or feed on the oozing body juices.

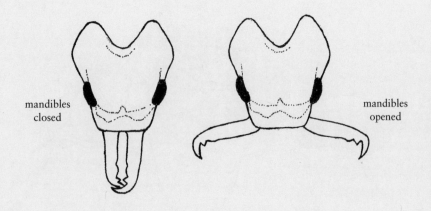

mandibles closed

mandibles opened

Trap-jaws of Daceton

Food flow within an ant colony

Foraging ants collect more food than they need for themselves, much of the excess food being passed to nurse workers that remain inside the nest. Food may also be passed in the opposite direction, from nurse workers to foragers if a forager returns hungry. Ants feed each other by regurgitation of liquid from the crop. Those species that do not have crops capable of storing liquids, such as species of the Ponerinae, may carry droplets of fluid between their jaws which are passed to nest mates. Workers returning from foraging trips may offer food and hungry workers may beg for food. In both cases

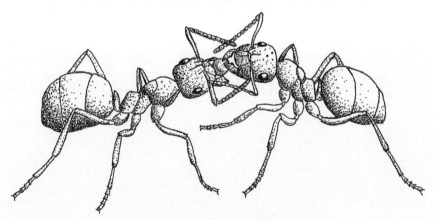

One worker feeding another (wood ant)

routine behavioural patterns are observed. Typical behaviour often involves a hungry ant lifting its head, while the forelegs are lifted off the ground, the antennae bent into an elbow. The jaws of the two ants are locked together, a drop of liquid appears on the tongue of the feeder (from the crop) and is passed into the mouth of the hungry ant. Begging ants will often stroke the heads and mouthparts of foragers with their forelegs and antennae to encourage the other ant to feed them.

LEAF SELECTION BY ANTS

Scientific studies have shown that leaf-cutting ants are very fussy about which leaves they select for cutting to take back to the nest. The decision by a worker to cut particular leaves depends on how tough the leaf is, how much water is contained inside the leaf and whether or not there are any chemicals present in the leaves that might kill them or the fungus. Young leaves and flowers are generally preferred because they contain fewer chemicals that are poisonous. However, there are many plants that contain substances that are toxic to fungi; how do the ants know which leaves to bring back to the nest that will not harm their fungus garden? Recent research has shown that it is likely that the fungus is able to communicate with the tiny worker ants that tend the fungus garden. If the foraging workers bring leaves for the fungus containing substances that are poisonous to the fungus, the fungus is thought to produce a chemical signal to say that it is not happy, which is detected by the gardening ants. The gardening ants somehow alert the foragers that the leaves that they are harvesting are no good for the fungus garden, the foragers then reject those leaves.

Feeding the larvae
In advanced species workers may feed the larvae mouth to mouth but it is doubtful that primitive species distribute food in this way. The fluid given to the larvae is a mixture of substances from various glands in the head containing enzymes to assist in the digestion of food, and chemicals which influence development of the larvae. This fluid is mixed with other foods like insect fragments or plant material from the crop of the workers.

The larvae are also fed on special eggs called 'trophic eggs'. These are different from reproductive eggs in that they are smaller and softer. Trophic eggs are laid by the workers but in species where workers lack ovaries (e.g. fire ants) the eggs are produced by the queen. The trophic eggs and larvae are often placed together in a pile, sometimes with reproductive eggs which are eaten also. Queen ants that are founding new colonies feed the larvae exclusively on trophic eggs to start with.

The workers normally chew up food material and place it on the mouthparts or in a feeding basket (a little pouch under the mouth on the thorax, formed from fleshy outgrowths or little hairs of the cuticle) when feeding the larvae. The food is placed in the basket and the larva helps itself. Harvester ant larvae (*Pogonomyrmex*) put their heads inside the basket to feed on bits of seed placed there by the nurse workers. In primitive species the larvae are carried inside the nest to the food which is usually freshly killed insects or other arthropods.

The larvae themselves may also play a role as a food store. In seed harvesting ants the workers place crushed seed on the head of the larvae, the material is ingested and regurgitated back to the workers after being digested. Larval secretions are consumed by both workers and queen, in fact the anal region of the larvae produces two kinds of fluid: a milky fluid which is relished by the workers, as it contains a mixture of digestive enzymes, and a clear fluid which is a waste product of the larvae and is quickly removed as a small droplet and disposed of outside the nest.

FORAGING AND TEMPERATURE

The daily foraging patterns of ants are influenced a great deal by the environment, particularly temperature and light. Many ants living in hot climates are prevented from foraging when the temperature outside the nest gets too high. In temperate regions low air temperatures may prevent some ants from foraging but as the day warms up more and more workers leave the nest. With wood ants there is a positive relationship between the internal temperature of the nest and the number of ants which leave the nest to forage: the higher the nest temperature the greater the number of ants foraging. There are of course species that are adapted to foraging at low temperature between 5° and 10° C. In spring, I found that wood ants (*Formica rufa*), in southern Britain, stop foraging when air temperature drops to about 7° C; numbers of ants outside the nest

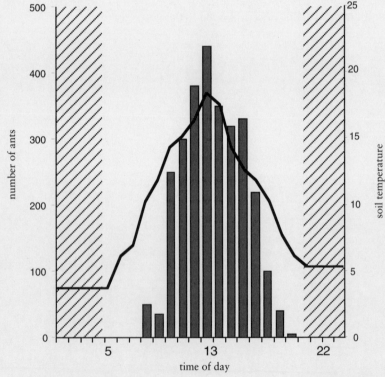

The number of wood ants running past a point on a foraging track in three minutes during a day in late April. The solid line indicates the temperature of the soil. Notice how ant activity follows closely soil temperature. Shaded area is night. (from R. North, 1993)

is greatest around 22°C. If the soil temperatures become too great at midday then few ants will leave the nest; most of the foraging occurs in the morning and late afternoon. In summer the numbers of wood ants foraging may be highest at night even though air temperature may be lower than during the day. There is scientific evidence that ants have an internal biological clock which governs the time of day when they are the most active outside the nest.

The daily foraging activities of ants in south-western Australia show remarkable precision in timing when the daytime foraging species of ants are replaced by night-time foraging ants at dusk. It is likely that ants have some innate sense of time to tell them when to become active and when to rest. In South America, leaf-cutting ants that forage during the day will appear at the entrance holes of their nest a few minutes before dawn ready to begin foraging.

Ant homes

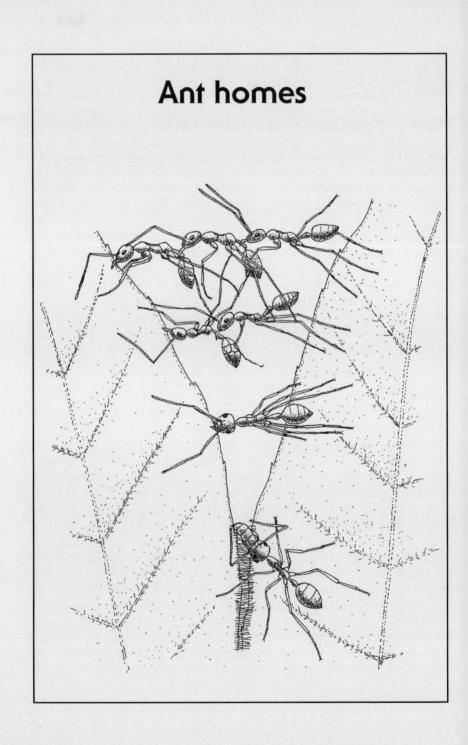

B ees and wasps must build special chambers inside their nests for rearing brood, whereas ants do not. The queen ant deposits her eggs in a pile on the floor of the nest. This enables ants to exploit a wide diversity of habitats for building different types of nests: in fact there are few places where ants do not build nests. Different species are adapted for living at the tops of trees, above ground, beneath ground, inside plant stems, in dead and living wood and buildings; ants even make homes out of the living bodies of their own species. Ants living in temperate climates, like that of Britain, must hibernate in their nests during the winter as it is too cold, but they will move around in warm wintry weather. Wood ants come to the surface of the nest to sunbathe in February on sunny days. But there would not be enough food available should they remain active all winter. Species of *Lasius* (which includes black garden ants) and wood ants (species of *Formica*) tend not to overwinter with brood; by the time winter arrives the brood have developed into adults. In contrast red ants (*Myrmica*) do overwinter with brood; final stage larvae, pupae and, of course, the brood remain in a state of hibernation and do not continue growing until the spring. The nest gives complete protection from an otherwise hostile environment, protection from predators, a place to rear brood during the spring and store food.

Ant-hills

Soil mounds are characteristic of those species of ant that live in the cool northern hemispheres like Britain. The mounds tend to buffer against sudden changes in temperature outside, remaining several degrees above air temperature and cooling more slowly at night. Many species that make soil mounds vacate them during the winter and move below ground. The yellow meadow ants (*Lasius flavus)* are familiar mound builders that live in open pasture land in Britain and move underground in winter; their ant-hills become covered with grass and small herbs and some may be hundreds of years old, and be indicative of ancient grasslands. As a general rule, the larger the ant-hill, the older it is. The mounds of earth are formed from soil excavated from beneath the hill; the ants scrape away the soil with their front legs and carry small pellets of soil, in their jaws, to the surface which produces a very fine tilth. A system of tunnels and galleries is made inside the mound. Some species of ants (*Formica fusca*) may add bits of vegetation such as stems and leaves to make the structure more durable.

A wood ant's nest is a remarkable piece of animal architecture. Wood ants build a hill or mound from pieces of vegetation (pine needles, small twigs or

Weaver ants using larvae as tubes of glue

leaf stems) which gives the impression of a thatched roof. The ants occupy galleries in the mound and soil beneath. The entrances to the nest are at the base of the hill. They also pile thatching onto decaying logs or into tree trunks; the workers then cut tunnels and galleries, with their jaws, into the decaying wood – hence the name wood ant. Other species that are related to wood ants (e.g. *Formica exsecta*) build soil mounds covered over with bits of vegetation. The thatching material is organised into a mound anything up

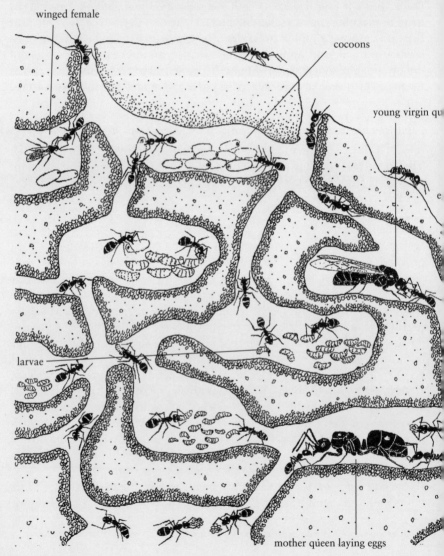

winged female

cocoons

young virgin qu

larvae

mother queen laying eggs

to 1.2 metres (4 feet) tall, but young nests may be very small, less than 30 centimetres (1 foot). As estate agents would be quick to point out, most wood ant nests have a south-facing aspect, with the south side of the mound usually shallower to increase the amount of surface area presented to the sun's rays. The hill acts like a solar panel, collecting energy from the sun and using it to heat the interior of the nest. Mounds that receive direct sunlight are shallow, whereas those in dense woodland are taller, so as to trap as much sunshine as possible. As with soil mounds, the thatching material has good insulating properties, holding heat. If the nest overheats the wood ants respond by opening small holes near the top of the mound. At night these holes are closed. The inside may be several degrees above the temperature of the air outside, the highest temperature being in the centre. In early spring the pupae are moved close to the surface of the mound where they are warmed

The activities of black garden ants inside a cutaway of their nest. The workers can be seen transporting eggs, larvae and cocoons. The cocoons are brought close to the surface of the nest where they are warmed by the heat of the sun. Other workers may be seen feeding the larvae and each other. The nest also contains winged ants; a young queen (the larger) and a smaller male ant. The mother queen can be seen at the bottom laying eggs which are collected by a worker as they come out.

workers

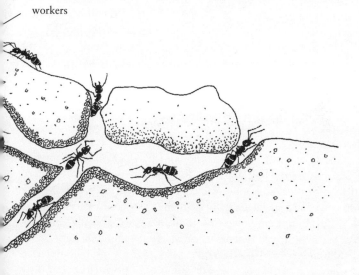

by the sun, which enhances the development to adults considerably. Very large nests may be heated by the workers who sunbathe on the surface of the mound, and then return to the centre of the mound to release the heat; thus the whole mound warms up from the inside. Below is a table showing some temperature measurements of wood ant nests I have taken at different times of the day:

Time of day	Air temp.°C	Nest temp. °C
21.00	17.9	29.0
5.00	13.5	24.9
9.00	14.4	22.6
12.00	14.0	20.3
16.00	16.0	22.0

Typical internal temperatures of a wood ant mound in August (at a depth of 12 centimetres /4.5 inches from the top of the mound).

The table above shows that the temperature inside the nest is several degrees higher than the outside – particularly at night. Even in winter when the temperature outside is 0°C I have measured nest temperatures between 3–5°C in some large nests. If an artificial mound is built of the same material but without ants, the internal temperature does not rise much above the external air temperature. The heating effect probably occurs because of the heat released from the bodies of the ants themselves, as a result of their cell metabolism. In living organisms much of the energy produced by the metabolism of food to produce energy is wasted as heat. Small wood ant mounds, housing only small populations of ants, do not reach very high temperatures inside simply because there are fewer ants producing heat. This can be a disadvantage: many small nests do not survive over the winter.

Underground nests
Nests that are constructed underground often open to the surface via tiny holes. Some nests may start in the soil layers and be extended into rotting logs and trees. Sometimes the soil which is dug out is deposited around the entrance as a little pile or crater. Some species of South American ants, which are closely related to the leaf-cutting ants (in that they cultivate a fungus garden, see p.47), but do not cut leaves, build little turrets, about 5 centimetres (2 inches) high, around the entrance of the nest from pieces of plant material and dead insects. Perhaps the turret serves as a kind of barrier to keep out unwelcome guests. These ants are small, with populations of only 50–100 workers.

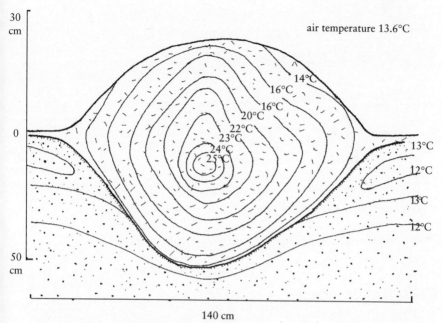

Temperature gradient inside a wood ant nest (after Dieter Coenen Stass et al, 1980)

Flat stones are very attractive to ants because they can burrow beneath. The soil may cool slower beneath a stone compared to the surrounding area, and stones radiate heat, particularly at night. European black and red garden ants excavate galleries under paving stones in towns and cities, cutting narrow tunnels horizontally beneath the paving slabs linking small chambers where the brood are reared. Other tunnels may lead to plant roots where aphids are feeding; the aphids supply the ants with honey-dew, which is an important source of energy (p. 49).

Garden ants are very sensitive to temperature changes and move their larvae around the nest to achieve optimal temperature ranges to speed their growth. If you lift a paving slab or stone in the garden that has been warmed by the sun it is not unusual to find hundreds of ants and their brood in little chambers beneath.

How deep into the soil a nest extends depends on how tolerant a species is likely to be of drought and heat. In the African savanna primitive ants like *Amblypone* go down to about 20 centimetres (8 inches), more advanced species such as *Camponotus* and *Pheidole* dig to a depth of 60 centimetres (24 inches). Ants that live in hot, arid environments tend to burrow deeper into the soil away from the surface, where it is cooler. Harvester ants (*Messor*),

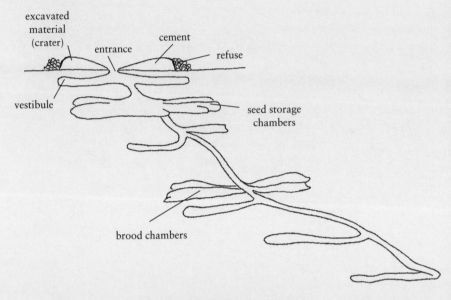

Underground nest of Messor

living in one of the hottest and most inhospitable environments in the world, Death Valley, excavate shafts several feet beneath the soil. The shaft has side branches leading into different chambers for housing the eggs, larvae and stored seeds. The entrances of the nests are betrayed by large craters at the soil surface made from sand granules cemented together by a yellowish cement. The periphery of the crater is surrounded by spent seed husks which the workers dump from inside the nest.

The most spectacular underground nests are constructed by leaf-cutting ants, which dig out huge cavities beneath the ground and pile the soil outside. The actual construction of the nest is quite complicated as it requires a cooling system to remove the heat generated from the fungus gardens. Without a proper cooling system the temperature of fungus chambers would rise and almost certainly kill the fungus, which is very sensitive to changes in temperature. The nest of the leaf-cutting ant is constructed in such a way that there is a ring of tunnels running horizontally around the nest: openings lead from this to the outside, so that the holes into the nest may be located some distance away. Branching from these horizontal tunnels are the fungal chambers of which there could be a hundred or so. Leaf pieces are stored in special chambers as they are brought into the nest before being used in the fungus garden. Other chambers may be used to dump refuse, mainly consisting of dead fungus, bodies of ants and waste. Ventilation shafts run vertically and terminate in small craters to the outside. The ventilation system is driven by the heat generated from the fungus garden; hot air rises up the shafts and is replaced by cooler air from outside. The fungus chambers of leaf-cutters (*Atta*) in Brazil are at about 25°C at all times of the day, never varying by more than 4° each way.

The nests of leaf-cutting ants can be enormous, with enough room for a man to stand up inside. Sometimes a nest dies and the whole structure becomes unstable, the soil subsides leaving a big hole. In Brazil many roads and highways are menaced by leaf-cutter ants nests along the margins. On some roads there is an average of 50 nests per half mile of road. Potentially on a 29 mile (46-kilometre) stretch around 46 cubic metres of soil could be removed by the ants. Quite often the ground gives way and large trucks find themselves in huge craters of what were once ants' nests!

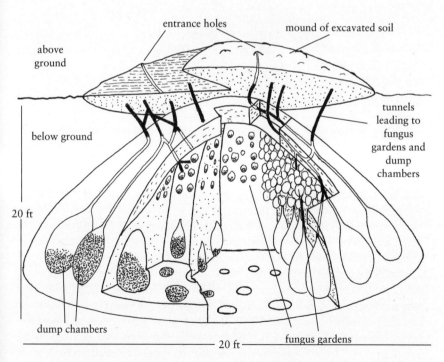

Leaf-cutter ant nest (after Jonkmann in Hölldobler and Wilson, 1990)

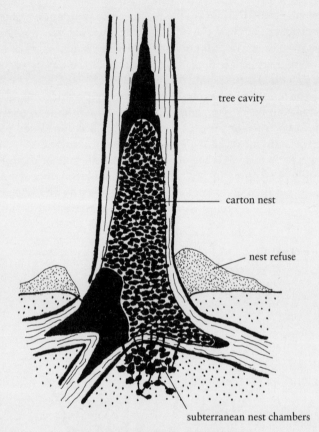

Carton nest of the shining black ant
(after Maschwitz and Hölldobler, 1970, in Hölldobler and Wilson, 1990)

Carton nests

Some ants build themselves a carton structure inside soil and wood cavities: it is a rigid structure, of any shape, with internal walls, rather like a sponge. Instead of using paper, these ants make the walls of the carton from chewed wood particles, plant matter and insect pieces stuck together by saliva or honey-dew which sets quite hard. An African species of *Crematogaster* may build a hundred or so carton nests in trees; each nest may be quite large – 30 by 25 centimetres (12 by 9 inches) and several centimetres may added to the nest each year. When a nest becomes too small new nests may be founded in the tree, all nests probably forming an interrelated colony. The European shining black ant (*Lasius fuliginosus*) creates a carton in which the structure

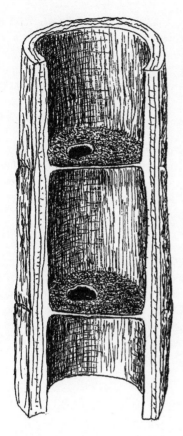

Cutaway nest of Aztecta *ants in bud or stem*

is supported by a fungus growing on the walls that divide the inside of the nest up into small cells (1–2 centimetres cubed). As far as is known the ants do not feed on the fungus. The addition of new building materials to the top of the carton provides the fungus with fresh substrate as it grows.

Ants that live in or on plants

Many species make nests in hollow stems of grasses and other herbs; examples are *Crematogaster impressa* on the Ivory coast or *Leptothorax* in Britain. *Leptothorax*, which are tiny ants, also live inside fallen acorns. Obviously the populations are very small and the home is only temporary as acorns do decay slowly. Species like *Camponotus* and *Pheidole* look after the larvae in hollow stems of grasses while the queen together with her eggs resides in the soil below. There are many ants that live in the trunks and branches of trees, cutting into dead and living wood. The large carpenter ants (*Camponotus herculeanus*) cut their way higher and higher inside a tree, perhaps 9 metres (30 feet) from the base of the trunk. In winter the ants move back down into the soil. Carpenter ants are found in North America, Scandinavia and most of Europe, Britain excepted. Occasionally wood ants may build a mound around a tree stump and actually invade the interior of the stump, filling it with a mass of holes rather like Swiss cheese. Wood ants may also build inside the hollow trunk of a dead tree filling the hollow with twigs or pine needles; the wood absorbs heat during the day and retains it throughout the night when the external air temperature can drop considerably.

The *Azteca* ants make their homes under bark or hollow stems. In South America the trumpet tree (*Cecropia*) is invaded by queen ants when it is quite small. The queen bites out the inside of the stem above a bud. When the workers come along they continue to eat away the interior of the stem so that as the tree grows the stem bulges out because of the weight of the tree above pushing down. Many different species of ant build carton nests in trees around the stems and buds. Debris soon starts to collect around the nest, which provides a soil for the germination of seeds of different types of plants known as epiphytes (epiphytes: plants which grow on other plants).

The leaf bases of palms growing in the Lamto savanna, Africa, are the home to many species of ants. The leaf bases become filled with soil particles and may house around 34,000 individual ants.

The rhizomes of an epiphytic fern (*Lecanopteris*) are home to five species of *Crematogaster* and *Iridomyrmex* (Australia to Southern Thailand). The ants build a carton inside the rhizomes, and the plant benefits from its tenants by absorbing the nutrients from the ant faeces through the rhizome wall. There are at least ten genera of tropical epiphyte that serve as homes for ants. The ants also defend their plant houses, and therefore the plant, from plant-eating animals. The *Acacia* tree is a well known ant-defended plant, one of its defendants being the ant *Pseudomyrmex*, which is very aggressive. The ants swarm from the plant as soon as they detect the scent of man or any other mammal that might be about to have a meal off the acacia leaves. The intruder is then covered in a mass of extremely painful stings. Other insects, including large beetles, are seen off. The tree, in fact, shelters many species of ant and provides them with sweet nectar from nectaries which are like little glands, occurring on the stems and leaves of many plants.

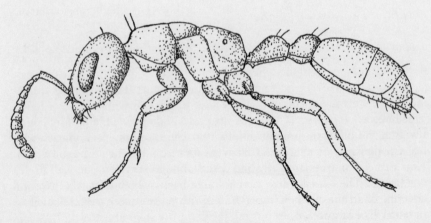

Pseudomyrmex

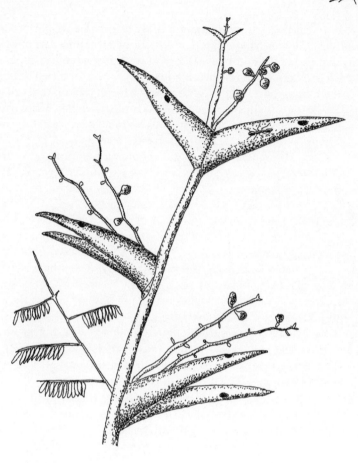

End of acacia branch, showing paired hollow thorns inhabited by Pseuydomyrmex

Tree houses

Living high up in trees presents another problem to ants – lack of moisture, because they may be a long way from the damp conditions of the soil below. Ants that live in trees are able, like desert ants, to survive quite well in dry conditions. They do not lose much water from their bodies, the external covering of an ant's body is impregnated with waxes which prevents the loss of water by evaporation.

The leaves of trees are also used by ants to create homes. The weaver ants

A bivouac

(*Oecophylla longinoda*) of tropical Africa and the green tree ants of Australia and the Far East (*Oecophylla smaragdina*) build carton nests from leaves which are held together by strands of silk, all the time still attached to the tree. The carton is made by folding over the edges and tips of leaves to make a tent-like structure. The threads of silk are produced from silk glands in the heads of the early stage larvae (final stage are too big for the ants to carry). The workers collect the larvae from nearby nests and carry them to the nest construction site. By waving the larvae back and forth, like a tube of glue, the folded leaves are secured. The nest entrances and galleries are often made entirely of silk and look rather like a spider's web. Construction work can be tricky: if the leaves are far apart a worker will have to stretch across the gap to reach the other leaf, or workers may climb on each other to make a bridge, one gripping the edge of the leaf with the hind legs to reach across, seizing with its jaws the petiole of the worker in front. The edge of one leaf is held by the jaws of the worker in front. They then all pull together and the gap between the leaves is closed. While workers pull the leaves together other workers are busy with the larval tubes of glue fastening the edges of the leaves with silken threads. The whole tree in which the ants build may be filled with more than a hundred of these carton nests.

Roving ants

Army ants would find a nest an unnecessary hindrance to their nomadic way of life so they make camp in a temporary nest called a bivouac made from their own bodies. After a raid (see p. 45) the ants form a cluster and link together by the tarsal claws on their feet to produce a closed bag several layers thick. The shape of the bag varies from a simple pouch to a cylinder or a plug in the hollow of a tree. The queen and the brood reside at the centre of the mass. The temperature at the centre is always a few degrees higher than that outside (about 24–28° C). In cool weather many of the ants leave the bivouac to sun themselves on rocks and when they return to the bivouac the heat released from their bodies raises the temperature inside.

ANT TOOLS

There are scientific reports of ants using 'tools' to transport food back to the nest. One report is of harvester ants (*Pogonomyrmex badius*) in Florida that drop grains of sand into pools of liquid food and carry the sand grains, covered with the food, back to the nest. In colonies of fire ants kept in a laboratory it took the workers about 48 hours to transport 1 millilitre of honey back to their nest using grass stalks and sand grains as 'tools'.

Ants in buildings

Ants that choose to live with man do so because of the warmer temperature of buildings. The most notorious is the pharaoh ant (*Monomorium pharaonis*); originally from Egypt, this ant is now able to survive in Britain because of central heating in hospitals, bakeries and blocks of flats. They are a serious problem in hospitals because of their potential to transmit disease (p.115). Nests may be made in a number of places inaccessible to humans, like boxed-in pipes, fuse boxes, light fittings, heating ducts and even automatic vending machines. The ants are able to travel around on man, food trolleys, linen and even nurses' cloaks!

Another ant that causes concern in hospitals is the Argentine ant (*Iridomyrmex humilis*); in one hospital corridor a foraging trail 15 metres (50 feet) long was recorded! Garden ants may visit the homes of man but in most cases it is just a foraging trail from the outside to a food source, such as jam left on a kitchen surface. Black ants usually nest outside but close to buildings; a trail of workers may enter the house through a hole in the brickwork or beneath a door. The brown tree ant *(Lasius brunneus)* is one species that normally lives in the trunk of old oak trees but on occasions may invade

YUK! I HATE HOSPITAL FOOD

the oak beams of older style dwellings and can extend its tunnelling activities into new wood, causing damage.

There is a rather interesting ant (*Hypoponera punctatissima*) which may be found, all the year round, in heated greenhouses. It nests in soil-filled pots and boxes, and was established by accident, being native to sub-tropical regions; it may live outside in Britain but only in very sunny locations.

How old are ant nests?

It is difficult to know how long ant nests can survive. Sometimes a colony may move to another nest, leaving the old one behind. If there is only one queen, as is the case for weaver ants and leaf-cutting ants, when she dies then that is the end of the colony. In captivity ant queens may live for 10 years or more. Army ant queens (*Eciton burchelli*) usually live for at least 5 years. A study made on the weaver ant (*Oecophylla longinoda*) living in palm trees showed that in a three-year period out of 165 colonies 11 died and 7 colonies moved out. After 5 years only 30% of the nests survived, most having been destroyed by other ants. The thatched mounds of *Formica ulkei* can continue for 20–25 years. Over a period of 6 years a total of 56 nests were monitored: 18 survived after 2 years and when the 6 years had passed only 13 nests were left. Of the British species, wood ant nests may survive up to 25 years; out of 18 nests of the yellow meadow ant, *Lasius flavus*, only 6 of them lived 8 years. The colonies were killed by red ants who feed on *Lasius flavus*. Changes in the habitat probably contributed to their demise.

WALL-PAPERING ANTS

Harpegnathos saltator or the wall-papering ant of India and SE Asia likes to wallpaper the inside of its nest. The inside of the nest chambers are lined with empty cocoons, insect debris and vegetable material glued together by a secretion from a special gland in the abdomen. It is doubtful that the function of the wallpaper is decorative but probably serves to control the moisture and temperature inside the chambers ideal for the growth of the brood.

The construction of the nest is rather unique, the ant builds a large sphere, from soil, below ground. A gap of about 6 mm is maintained between the sphere and the surrounding soil except for where it rests on the soil at the bottom. Inside the sphere there are a series of horizontal chambers where the brood is kept and chambers for dumping rubbish. The ants enter the chambers through reinforced openings in the floors and ceilings. The function of the sphere may be to prevent the main part of the nest from flooding during the monsoon season. Water dripping through the soil from the surface would run into the cavity surrounding the sphere and drain away keeping the central part of the nest dry.

How ants find
their way home

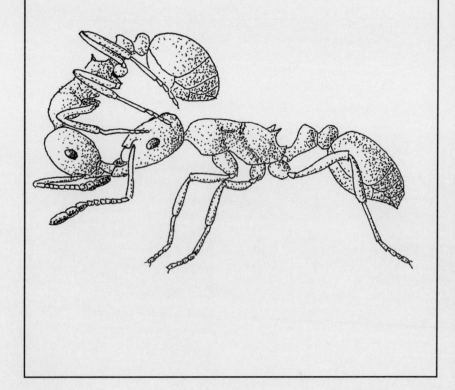

S ome ants, including those that live in British gardens and towns, never venture more than about 4 or 5 metres (13 or 16 feet) from the nest. Other ants such as wood ants may go as far as 200 metres (218 yards). How do ants find their way home? There are several answers: the most obvious is by scent or pheromone trails; scent trails do not last very long as the substance eventually evaporates. The method of navigating used depends on the situation in which an ant may find itself; there is always a back-up method should one fail. Ants may make use of the shape of the land or landmarks, the position of the sun in the sky, shape of the tree canopy above the nest – even magnetic fields and 'odour landscapes' have been suggested by entomologists.

Ant motorways

Wood ants have well trodden routes which lead them from the nest to places where they usually find food. Wood ant tracks can be clearly seen as they pass through the undergrowth in British woodlands. Some tracks might be half a metre wide, ant motorways carrying hundreds of foraging worker ants to the hunting grounds. Often these trails follow man-made paths because they are conveniently clear of vegetation which would otherwise hamper the flow of traffic.

Leaf-cutting ants of the New World also have permanent tracks which radiate outwards from a central nest; the route taken by the foraging workers is obvious where the vegetation is worn away by thousands of marching ant feet. Other species of ants have specialised workers to remove plant roots and debris to keep the foraging tracks open.

Foraging wood ants always stick to the same route every day, and the same pathways may be used year after year. Entomologists have marked individual wood ant workers with spots of paint (which cause them no harm and soon come off) and found that individuals from different parts of a nest always go along the same paths. The exact foraging routes are passed on from generation to generation of worker ants. Memory of the routes will be maintained by natural selection (**see p.11**), if they always lead to food.

Navigation by landmarks

How do wood ants know which route to take? Some ants, wood ants in particular, have very good vision and studies have shown that they navigate by landmarks – for example groups of trees or rocks which tell the workers that they are getting closer to the nest. This has been proven by scientific studies: when a small area of woodland surrounding a wood ant nest is cleared of a few trees sufficient to change the landscape, then the ants, which

Leptothorax *carrying a nest mate*

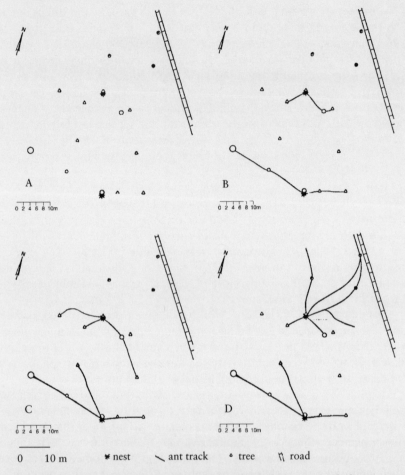

Seasonal enlargement of foraging areas from nests: A shows ant trails from nests in March; B in April; C in May and D shows how many trails they are making in August (after Mabelis, 1973)

are identified by marking, which normally stick to certain routes, become disorientated. Wood ants can also be trained to navigate by an artificial landmark like a lamp or black disc. When using landmarks, ants obviously use their eyes – made up of 100 or so facets or tiny lenses. When navigating the ant always maintains the image of the landmark on a group of lenses in the middle of the eye so that the ant walks in a straight line. The ant appears to hold the image as a memory.

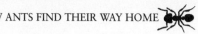

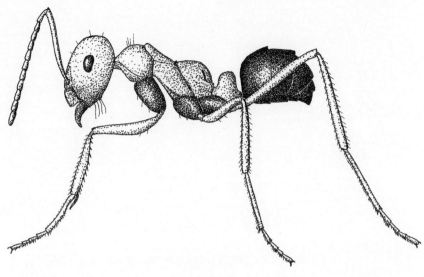

Cataglyphis

The desert ant (*Cataglyphis*), which is native of the Mediterranean region, North Africa and the Near East, always returns to the same place where it has caught prey before. Again, scientific research has shown that these ants are able to remember more than one location where they were successful at finding food. If they fail to find food in one place they navigate to another. How do they do this? Research has shown that when they leave the nest they take an almost straight path directly to the hunting grounds, but adopt a rather meandering route as they search for food. It appears that they remember sequences of landmarks, like a photograph, which appear one after another as the worker proceeds to and from home. Furthermore, when landmarks are not visible they rely on a system of dead reckoning by knowing the direction in which they travel and the distance over different segments of the path they had taken – it's simple arithmetic: they add up the distances over each segment, calculate the average distance (mean vector) reverse their direction by 180° and head for home!

Pheromone trails

Pheromone or scent trails may be the most popular method that many ants use to locate their nests; harvester ants (*Pogonomyrmex badius*), for example, prefer to rely on scent trails rather than visual cues. In other species scent trails may act as a back-up method when the visual system is obscured. A visual system using landmarks works fine during daylight but how do ants

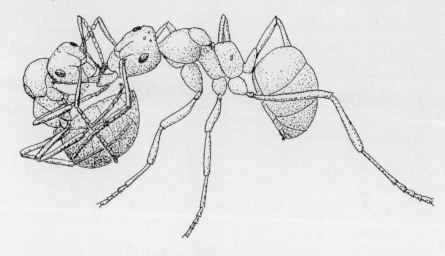

Young workers being transported

find their way at night? Wood ants (*Formica polyctena*) use landmarks during the day to keep to familiar routes, but at night they probably rely on scent trails. They run slower at night than during the day as they explore the ground, probably searching for scent trail. In the light it has been calculated that the workers run, on average, at a speed of 240 mm per second and in darkness at 170mm per second. Different routes may have different smells which are related to the type of food available on various foraging trails – a sort of 'odour landscape'.

The Amazon ant (*Polyergus breviceps*) is a species that invades other ant nests and carries away the brood (p.98). The scout ants find the nests by using visual cues, the sun and polarised light, backed up by trail pheromones. Research has shown that it is the more experienced scouts that use visual mechanisms to locate the nests of their intended victims, whereas inexperienced Amazon ant workers depend more on chemical trails.

It seems that young ants must learn to navigate using the different systems. Newly hatched workers often get lost. If one watches foraging wood ants in early spring many workers will be seen carrying another worker in their jaws; an ant being transported is carried with with legs folded beneath its head as if it were dead. Only it is not dead. It will be a young or naive worker which has got lost and is being returned to the nest by an older, more experienced, worker ant.

Using the sun to navigate
Many ants use the position of the sun relative to their nest to navigate home. On leaving the nest, desert ants (*Cataglyphis*) take a meandering path away

from the nest but a direct route back; all the while they keep at a constant angle to the sun. This is demonstrated by a simple experiment in which the sun is shielded on one side and reflected in a mirror on the other side. The ant will then reverse its direction by 180° and continue in the opposite direction to home. If the mirror is removed and the sun is visible again the ant proceeds in the correct direction home. However, the sun does not remain in the same position in the sky throughout the day, it moves 15° every hour. Ants are able to compensate for the sun's movement because they have an internal clock which computes where the sun should be at different times of the day. Scientific experiments on *Cataglyphis* show that when workers are placed in a dark box so they cannot see the sun they are still able to orientate themselves in the direction where they would expect the sun to be at that particular time of day.

Tree canopy orientation

The pattern created by the canopy of trees above ground was quite recently discovered, by entomologists, as yet another mechanism by which ants find their way home. The African stink ant (*Paltothyreus tarsatus*)(so called because it lets out a horrible stench when threatened) leaves its underground nest through an exit which is directly beneath the tree canopy so it cannot see the sky or the position of the sun. What it does is learn the pattern of the tree branches and leaves above it – a canopy pattern can easily be observed if one lays back and looks up directly into a tree. The canopy pattern is a bit like a map and the ant is able to make a 'mental picture' of the canopy to

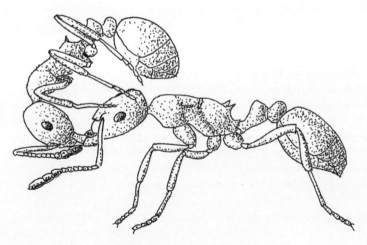

Leptothorax carrying a nest mate

work out the exact location of its nest. Bees use a similar mental map of the pattern of polarised light through an overcast sky.

Orientation to gravity

It is an advantage for ants to know whether they are travelling up or down. Ants are able to detect changes in gravity by special sensory hair plates in the neck, waist and leg joints. As the joints in the exoskeleton (the outer covering of the insect, onto which muscles are attached) are compressed when the body bends the little hairs are flattened and a nerve impulse is sent to the ant's brain. Therefore an ant knows what position its body is in. Wood ants walking up a vertical disc, which is slowly rotated, can be trained to maintain a constant angle of only 2° to gravity if food is placed at the edge of the disc. When red garden ants are disturbed on a plant stem they make their downward escape by orientating themselves to gravity. When they run on a horizontal surface they may orientate to light.

Orientation to magnetic fields

There is good scientific evidence that insects are receptive to magnetic fields. Many insects – bees, wasps and termites – show disturbances in their activity patterns or alter the direction in which they build their nests when they are placed in a magnetic field. The 'waggle dance' performed by bees to inform other bees of the whereabouts of food is not perfect and does contain some errors or mistakes about the position of the food, because the bee corrects for the position of the sun and the angle of gravity. These only appear as errors to human observers, the bees that leave the nest in search of the food are not affected by them. However, when the hive is exposed to an artificial magnetic field the dancing bee makes fewer mistakes. Particles of magnetite or 'lodestone' have been discovered in the abdomens of bees and many other insects, particularly those that migrate over long distances. One example is the monarch butterfly (*Danus plexippus*) which migrates a great distance from North America to the warmer South.

So far magnetic particles have not been found in ants, but they certainly respond to electrical and magnetic fields. Many ants are attracted to electrical contacts in transformers and electrical sockets. Wood ants appear to have the ability to orientate along the geomagnetic pole of the earth as well as the north pole of a magnet. The ability of fire ants (*Solenopsis invicta*) to lay a scent trail to food in a laboratory is made more difficult when the worker ants are exposed to a magnetic field which is suddenly reversed electrically. They take much longer to lay the trail than when the magnetic field remains unchanged.

Defence posture of the wood ant

Ants into battle

Ants are notorious for being war-like and aggressive. With an armoury of chemical weapons they should be taken seriously. Such weapons include jets of formic acid, an exploding abdomen and a sting containing protein-digesting venom. In addition ants may have powerful jaws, some with high-speed trigger mechanisms which are able to snip off a leg or head in a flash. Not all ants possess these weapons, indeed, some may have very few and depend on behavioural rituals or running away to get them out of trouble!

Most ants, however, will defend territory to the death in order to crush competition from other colonies. The vast numbers of worker ants and in some species soldier ants make them formidable opponents in battle.

Territorial behaviour

Wood ants are a good example of a species that supports large territory. The area of territory held by the red wood ant (*Formica rufa*) ranges from 272 square metres (325 square yards) to 1,616 square metres (1,930 square yards). The wood ant's territory often includes several nests grouped together, each nest being in communication with its neighbour by foraging tracks. Often workers will go from one nest to another bringing food and building materials. Other species of wood ants may have isolated nests and prefer not to be on friendly terms with their neighbours.

In a newly established wood ant nest the territory held by the population is small to begin with, but as the population grows there is a need for more food so they soon start to expand their territory. I have known the territory of wood ants to include the inside of people's cottages that are built at the edge of woodland! Sooner or later one colony meets up with another colony and that's when trouble starts. Spring battles between rival wood ant colonies occur because of a shortage of fly and other insect larvae, an important source of protein at this time of year. The battles usually cease later in the season when insect larvae become more abundant; then rival colonies may just about tolerate each other. Laboratory studies have shown that wood ants fed on a diet that contains very little protein become aggressive.

Other territorial war-like ants are the weaver ants (*Oecophylla*). Around twenty weaver ant nests can occupy a single tree and the territory of a weaver ant population may include twenty or so trees, which in tropical rainforest could mean land of 400–1,500 square metres (478–1,790 square yards). The nests may occupy one complete side of the tree, the side chosen depending perhaps on the direction of the wind or position of the sun, as the ants change sides with the season. Weaver ants defend their territory relentlessly against other weaver ants from different colonies (originating from a different queen) and other species of ants, although some species are tolerated and

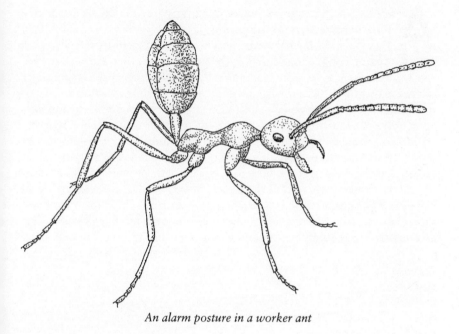

An alarm posture in a worker ant

may co-exist with the weaver ants providing they stay at ground level – the trees belong to the weavers!

The weavers construct battle stations on the edges of their territory which are constantly patrolled by workers. The battle stations are leaf nests (p.71), which house guards; they are the front line and prevent enemy ants from penetrating the nest in the interior of the territory. If an enemy was successful at knocking out these outposts then, on reaching the interior, it would be swamped by a second wave of workers and, hopefully for the weavers' sake, the enemy would be rapidly destroyed.

Battle tactics

The moment an alien is found wandering in the territory of another species or colony of ants the colony becomes alarmed. The alarm is raised by an alarm pheromone or scent produced by the worker that has discovered the intruder. When alarmed, workers adopt a typical posture of open jaws and raised front of the body or abdomen (see above). The intruder may then be attacked and the fighting ants produce more alarm pheromone which summons other workers to the battle site. During the battle the enemy ants may be seized by the legs or antennae; a worker under attack usually remains motionless as the other ants chop it to pieces. The dead and dying are carried to a rubbish dump or back to the nest to be eaten.

Fire ants (*Solenopsis*) find their food in the territory of the ant *Pheidole dentata*; taking the line that attack is the best method, they are very aggressive to their mortal enemies. Consequently *Pheidole* has evolved some very interesting battle tactics in the event of an attack by fire ants. *Pheidole* territory begins at some distance from the nest. If a small number of fire ants enter *Pheidole* territory while foraging for food, *Pheidole* minor workers will engage the enemy. As they approach the fire ants they lay scent trails by dipping the hind ends of their abdomens onto the ground. The volatile chemicals making up these trails will recruit 'soldier' ants or major workers from the surrounding area to finish the fight. On their arrival the soldiers begin snipping the fire ants to pieces with their powerful jaws. If on the other hand the number of invading fire ants is much greater and fighting extends as far as *Pheidole's* nest, the minors lay fewer scent trails and the fire ants meet

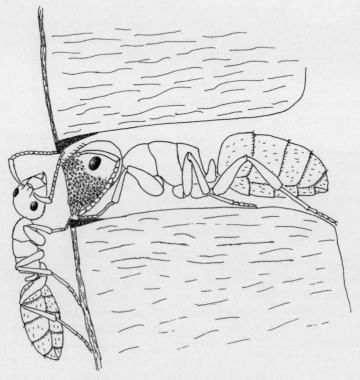

Ant head used to plug entrance of nest

with *Pheidole* soldiers already in the nest. If the battle continues to go badly for *Pheidole* some of the minor workers return to the nest to retrieve eggs and larvae which they carry to a safe place. Even the *Pheidole* queen makes a run for it, pushing through hordes of fighting ants. When the battle is over and the fire ants have left the battlefield *Pheidole* returns to the nest with the eggs, brood and queen.

External armour

As with most insects ants have a tough external skeleton which protects them to a certain degree from serious damage. In addition some species have spines and other strange protrusions to protect them. The head or abdomen may be flattened, like a shield, to prevent damage to more vulnerable areas. An ant found in the Brazilian Amazon (*Pheidole embolopyx*) has a queen with a flattened posterior which protects her from attack when she wedges herself into a tight crevice with her flat posterior facing the attackers.

In some species the major workers have massive heads and thoraxes which serve to plug the entrance of the nest (see opposite). The major workers act like doors and only pull back to open the door to those workers that have the correct smell and behaviour. If the doorway is very large then it could take several workers to plug it! Instead of using their heads, some ants prefer to use their abdomens which are heavily armoured. A West Indian ant (*Zacryptocerus varians*) has major workers with heads shaped like the oblique blades of bulldozers on enlarged thoraxes. The ants live in the trunks of dead trees where their shape makes them ideal for blocking the nest entrances. The bulldozer heads are also well shaped for pushing intruders out of the nest; the minor workers warn the majors of approach-

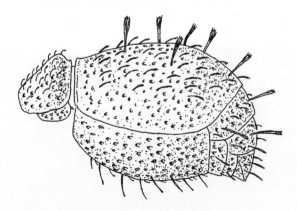

Hairs that fix debris to ant's body

ing foes who are bulldozed from the nest. If they prove to be difficult customers the majors join forces and squeeze the intruders out!

The heads of *Zacryptocerus* major workers are covered with bits of debris so that they are more difficult to spot in the nest entrance. Camouflage is used by quite a few species of ant to prevent them from being seen by enemies. Some tropical species have bizarre hair-like structures all over their bodies which collect the soil particles to camouflage them. Special hairs known as 'brush' hairs collect the particles, and other 'holding' hairs fix them to the ant's body (see illustration p.87). When covered with soil particles, they look like blobs of mud, very difficult to see. Only workers that forage outside the nest make use of camouflage, the young workers that remain inside the nest are shiny.

Other ants prefer to be seen, so they are very brightly coloured. This warning colouration, as with bees and wasps, warns predators that they are not a push-over and can defend themselves, usually with a very powerful sting. The Australian bull or jumping ants are good examples: they have very bright metallic colours and an extremely nasty sting combined with the ability to jump out of harm's way.

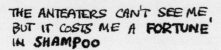

Jaws

The jaws of ants are used for both offence and defence. Sickle-shaped jaws are useful for piercing, and army ant soldiers line the raiding columns of marching ants with their sickle-shaped jaws pointing outwards, ready to take a lunge at anything that passes by.

Other ants have jaws engineered for shearing; such jaws are associated with large face muscles, capable of generating enough force to shear off or crush the antennae, leg or head of an opponent. Leaf-cutting ant soldiers have very large heads which consist mainly of muscle!

Some ants have what is known as a trap-jaw mechanism, an essential of which is extreme speed. The tropical species, *Odontomachus*, has the fastest reflex mechanism in the whole of the arthropod group (insects, spiders, crabs,

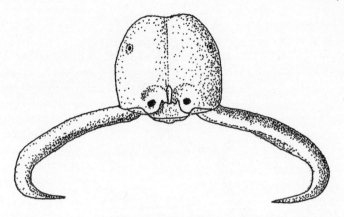

Sickle jaws of army ants

shrimps, etc.). The entire reflex action takes 4–10 milliseconds and the jaws close in less than 0.5 milliseconds. *Odontomachus* stalks its victim with its jaws, which are just under 2mm long, held open in a cocked state like a catapult with the elastic drawn back on the point of release. When the victim brushes against trigger hairs located on the jaws, these hairs cause the jaws to unlock, releasing the enormous amount of energy stored in the head capsule, and the jaws snap shut very fast. Special equipment used to photograph and make measurements show that the jaws actually slow down just before they collide to prevent self-inflicted damage should they miss their victim.

The sting

Many ants, mainly those species that are not very advanced, are equipped with stings. In Britain red garden ants are capable of delivering a very painful sting to humans. The sting, which is thought to have evolved from the long tube (ovipositor) used for laying eggs, consists of a long shaft, strengthened with heavy duty insect cuticle (similar to the outer exoskeleton of an insect) and supported by a lancet used for piercing the victim. The sharp bit of the sting protrudes from the end of the abdomen and the other end is inside connected to a poison sac by a tiny tube; the venom is pumped down the shaft from the sac into the victim. The sting is also joined to the Dufour's gland, and therefore has other functions, apart from stinging, like laying scent trails.

The venom often contains substances capable of killing small insects and breaking down animal tissue. The venom of bull ants have an additional chemical called histamine which, apart from producing pain, causes intense irritation to humans. The burning sensation produced by the sting of fire

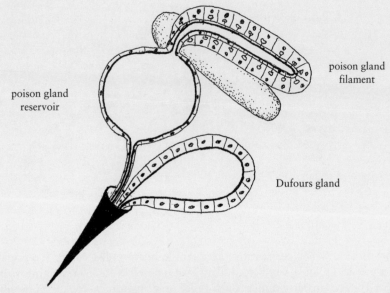

General anatomy of an ant sting

ants is due to alkaloid piperidines, substances not usually found in animals.

Chemical warfare

The sting of an ant generally has two functions, firstly, to immobilise prey or a threatening intruder, killing it, and, secondly, to release an alarm pheromone to alert nest mates of possible danger. The alarm pheromone prepares the workers for battle, a response that causes the workers to open their jaws and move towards the source of the alarm. Alarm pheromones are short-lived so they must be continually reinforced by fighting ants which are attacking the intruder; more and more ants begin to sting or bite the intruder so releasing more and more alarm pheromone. The alarm pheromone diffuses through air and is capable of alerting ants over a short distance, say 10 centimetres (4 inches). It finally dies away if not reinforced.

Alarm pheromones work at very low concentrations and can produce different behavioural effects in ants. A concentration of about 10^{10} molecules per centimetres^3 causes harvester ants (*Pogonomyrmex*) to become very aggressive and enter a state of frenzy, seeking to destroy any intruders in its nest. *Lasius alienus* on the other hand interprets alarm pheromones from 10^7 to 10^{10} molecules per centimetres^3 as an early warning of attack which gives it time to evacuate its nest.

Alarm pheromones are released from several sources – various glands in the head (mandibular glands) and gaster (Dufour's gland) – as well as the sting. Fire ants in battle release alarm pheromones from the head to excite other nest mates to join them in battle, and the Dufour's gland produces a trail pheromone which is deposited by the sting to lead the others to the battle site. Alarm pheromones are mainly hydrocarbons and ketones: 4–methyl–3–heptone is a common one. Another is undecane, which also serves as a mate attractant in wood ants: let us hope that there is no resulting confusion in signals (p.40).

We have seen that in advanced ants the sting loses its function as a weapon and is used to deposit pheromone. In the subfamily of ants Formicinae, the sting is replaced by a small pore which sprays formic acid. The 'acid pore', as it is called, is highly functional in the wood ants, and it sprays formic acid both as an alarm pheromone and in defence. Wood ants when threatened adopt a typical defence posture by pulling the gaster forward between the hind legs to spray jets of formic acid at the enemy. The spray also contains undecane which is a wetting agent and helps the acid to spread over the victim's body and be absorbed. Ants can even be killed by their own formic acid in a confined space like a jam jar. The acid pore is surrounded by a ring of little hairs to hold back droplets of acid so that they do not contaminate the rest of the ant's body.

Pheidole biconstricta is capable of expelling a pungent sticky liquid from a large gland (pygidial gland) in the abdomen in response to a frontal attack. The substance is forced out by contractions of the abdomen, and generally the smell is enough to repel attacking ants but if this fails the viscosity of the substance increases when exposed to air and makes the attacking ant very sticky; *Pheidole* makes its escape while its assailant tries to clean itself up.

Kamikaze ants
Camponotus saundersi is a walking 'bomb'. The mandibular glands of this ant extend from its head, down through its body into the abdomen. If the workers are attacked they squeeze their abdomen until it bursts, the mandibular glands also rupture and release a yellowish sticky fluid and attacking ants find themselves literally stuck up and unable to move! By dying for their colony kamikaze ants are an excellent example of altruism (see p.26).

The offensive
The thief ant (*Solenopsis fugax*) is a European species that steals the brood from other ant colonies by tunnelling into the nest chambers. When inside, the thief ant scouts lay a chemical trail from the Dufour's gland all the way back to their own nest to alert nest mates. As the raid takes place the thief ant releases an alkaloid venom from the poison gland. The venom repels the

Defence posture of wood ant

nurse workers of the raided nest so they cannot protect their brood. The thief ants can then steal the brood with ease.

Socially parasitic ants use pheromones from the Dufour's to mask the recognition chemicals of the host workers so they do not recognise each other. These are known as 'propaganda' pheromones and cause the host workers to attack each other. More will be said about this in the section on social parasitism (p.97).

Enemies of ants

Apart from insects and spiders, ants have many enemies in the form of birds and mammals. The winged ants become the prey of birds such as swifts, swallows, sparrows, even seagulls. Wood ants are a favourite of the green woodpecker. Some birds will pick up wood ants and squeeze them in their beaks before placing them under their feathers; the formic acid from the ants may serve to rid the birds of parasites such as fleas or ticks.

Many mammals, including man (p.116), enjoy ants as food. These mammals include the anteaters and armadillos of South America and the African aardvark. Australia has its share of ant-eating mammals such as the banded anteater and the porcupine. Wild chimpanzees use sticks, twigs and grass stems as tools to get ants out of the nest. They push the stick down an ant hole and leave it for a few seconds before taking it out. The stick comes out covered with ants which the chimp licks clean!

'BOXING' ANTS

A Japanese harvester ant (*Messor aciculatus*) goes in for martial arts. This species of harvester ant has no territorial boundaries as such. Nests are so close together that confrontations between neighbouring ants occur on a regular basis. If they fought to the death at every meeting it would be very costly in terms of energy, more and more workers would have to be produced, just to be killed in battle. So when workers from one colony returning from a foraging expedition meet workers from another colony, the weakest are robbed of their seeds. Dominant workers grab seeds from the jaws of other ants and carry the seeds back to their own nest. More often neighbouring colonies rob each others' nests of seeds.

Hostile encounters are very frequent near the nest entrances. Two hostile workers will turn and face each other, their jaws wide open and antennae touching; then they stretch out their forelegs and 'box' for up to a minute. Afterwards, they part and go their separate ways, the victor bearing the trophy of seed. On occasions the conflict escalates so that they bite each other. They may even start pulling one another and the winner could drag the loser over quite a distance before releasing it. They never injure each other though. This combat is a ritual in which no one is actually injured, but even so it may interfere with foraging or nest building activities of workers from neighbouring colonies to such an extent that some colonies are weakened because they are unable to collect enough food. The combat rituals usually end in the weaker colony being robbed of all its stored seeds and brood.

Ant parasites and slaves

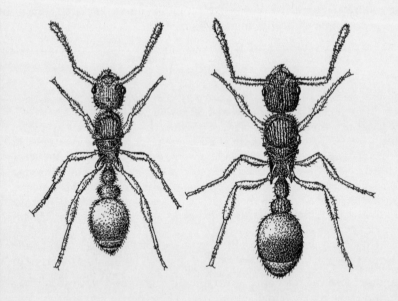

There are several associations in which ants exploit each other which may be termed parasitic. There is the temporary parasitic situation which has already been mentioned on p.42 where a queen invades the colony of a different species and uses the host workers to raise her brood. This gives rise to a mixed colony of host and parasite, though eventually the host workers die out leaving only the parasitic species which no longer requires the services of the other species, hence the term 'temporary'. There are some species which begin new colonies in this way but continue to enslave workers of the host species. Finally, there are permanent parasitic associations where one species actually lives in the nest of the host and is provided with food and shelter. There are of course the more loose parasitic relationships where a parasite might live in a nest next to its host, stealing food by following the scent trails of other ants to their food resources. Thief ants plunder the nests of other ants to steal brood to be consumed as food. Another method is to ambush foraging workers of another species and steal items of food they might be transporting.

Evolution of parasitism in ants

An interesting feature of parasitic and slave associations in ants is that the parasite is always very closely related to the host species – they have a recent ancestor in common. Parasitism among ants probably came about when two populations of ants which continued to grow and multiply in isolation (isolated possibly because they could not come together and mate for various reasons) were later reunited. They would have become genetically dissimilar but close enough to share certain characteristics like pheromone chemistry. This is very important particularly if a parasitic queen is to enter and maintain control over a host colony; as we shall see, having similar pheromone substances is a distinct advantage to the parasite.

Ant slavery may have evolved from one ant species preying on the brood of another, like the thief ants. It may be that the brood was taken into the nest and some pupae remained uneaten. These pupae hatched into young workers which took their place in the society of the fostering ants. This does not, however, explain temporary parasitic associations, because in this case the parasite is 'pretending' to be the prey; it seems more likely that slavery evolved from the need of some queens to employ other ants, even of a different species, to raise their brood.

True parasitic ants cannot survive without the host species, in fact the parasitic ant may regress into a condition where the behaviour and external structure of the parasitic ant is weakened because it relies entirely on its

Myrmica hirsuta inquilinous *sp and queen of host* Myrmica sabuleti

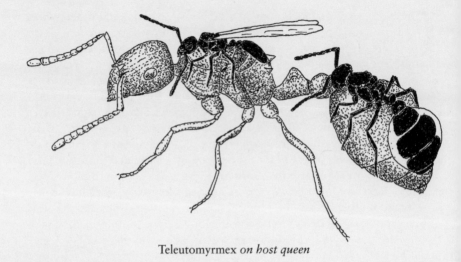

Teleutomyrmex *on host queen*

host. For example the glands inside the head are small, as parasitic ants no longer need to communicate a great deal with each other; the jaws weak and the sting is useless. Some parasitic ants may have no need for a nuptial flight as mating takes place inside the host nest. The reproductive ants are often very small so that more virgin queens can be produced without much energy expenditure; a large number of queens will have a greater chance of finding new hosts than just a few large ones, which would be more expensive in terms of energy.

Look no workers!
Many parasitic species have dispensed with workers altogether. The queen of *Teleutomyrmex schneideri*, found in central Europe, is only 2.5mm in length and rides on the body of its host – a *Tetramorium* queen. It makes frequent trips to the head end of the host to share the host queen's food. The *Teleutomyrmex* parasitic queens have undergone a number of external structural changes over millions of years, to adapt them to living on the surface of another ant. The feet have evolved to be large enough to anchor the parasite onto the host and the gaster is concave so that the parasite can press firmly against the host's body. *Teleutomyrmex* lays eggs in the host nest, the brood are mixed with the brood of the host and are cared for by the host workers. *Tetramorium* is somehow prevented from producing sexuals itself. Virgin queens mate with males inside the host nest and after fly out to find new *Tetramorium* nests.

Strongylognathus is another parasitic ant that has just queens without

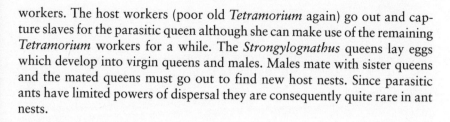

workers. The host workers (poor old *Tetramorium* again) go out and capture slaves for the parasitic queen although she can make use of the remaining *Tetramorium* workers for a while. The *Strongylognathus* queens lay eggs which develop into virgin queens and males. Males mate with sister queens and the mated queens must go out to find new host nests. Since parasitic ants have limited powers of dispersal they are consequently quite rare in ant nests.

Deception

On entering the host nest the parasite, be it a slave raider or a permanent parasite, must break through the defence system of the colony and, in the case of many permanent parasites, kill the host queen. As mentioned above, similarities in chemistry makes this easier as the host colony is likely to recognise the parasitic queen as their own, once the host queen has been destroyed. Entering the host colony can be done without aggression: for example, the parasitic queen of the dark guest ant *(Anergates atratulus)* plays dead outside the host colony. A host worker soon investigates the 'corpse'; the parasitic queen suddenly latches onto the curious worker's antenna with her jaws and is eventually dragged into the nest by the worker. Problems begin once the parasitic queen is inside the host nest for she must smell exactly like the host colony. Some parasitic queens will cover themselves in the chemical odour of an unfortunate host worker which she kills for the purpose of obtaining the colony scent. *Leptothorax kutteri*, which is a parasite of *Leptothorax acervorum*, secretes a 'propaganda' pheromone which causes the host workers to attack each other and in the confusion the parasitic queen is soon recognised as the one and only queen. *Harpagoxenus* also produces a kind of 'propaganda' pheromone which drives away all the host workers so that only the brood remains. The pupae soon hatch into workers who are then enslaved.

Ant slavery

The British Isles has its very own slave-making ant, the red slave-making ant *(Formica sanguinea)*. However, it does not totally depend on having slaves, it can survive quite happily making use of its own workers. The red slave ant prefers *Formica rubifarbis* or *Formica fusca* as slaves but on occasions it will take wood ants *(Formica rufa)*. Again, all these species are closely related to the red slave-making ant.

Like the wood ant, the red slave-making ant is territorial and very aggressive; it goes on raiding parties to capture slaves. Raids begin in the early morning, the party returning by sunset. First, the scouts locate the nest to be raided, which may be 50–100 metres (164–300 feet) away from the slave-making ants' nest. The slave-making ants usually leave in small parties and meet up close to the intended host nest. Naturally the host is soon alerted and may try to defend its nest and remove the brood to a safe place. The red slave-making ant workers do not often kill the host workers unless they put up much resistance, they carry the host brood back to their own nest. When the brood mature into workers they become slaves. The workers of the slave-making ants and slaves often work together nest building, cleaning and doing brood care duties but the slaves do not forage or go on slave raids. All in all the life of a slave is not too unpleasant.

The Amazon ants (*Polyergus*) of Europe and America conduct their slave raids in a different way to the red slave-making ants. After a scout ant alerts the colony to a good source of slaves the Amazon workers rush out in a great wave, raid the host nest and quickly return with the brood. It has been recorded that 2,000 Amazon ants raided a host colony (*Formica* spp.) 75 metres (246 feet) away, and returned with around 400 larvae and pupae. The Amazon workers have huge jaws which are used for piercing the bodies of the defending *Formica* workers during the slave raid. The Amazon raiders also produce chemicals which mimic the pheromone substance undecane, produced by *Formica* workers, which causes mass panic among the defenders; this allows the Amazon ants to penetrate the nest and steal the brood.

Lodgers or guests

Even the most aggressive ants share their homes with other creatures as guests or lodgers. Some lodgers are invited, while others enter the nest by deception. Many do not bother the ants at all but some may be hostile. Guests include other ants, beetles, flies, butterflies, spiders, scorpions, mites, woodlice, centipedes and millipedes.

Wherever ants build nests there is always somebody willing to move in with them because the nest provides a stable environment, food and shelter. The chambers usually contain either eggs, larvae, pupae, food or refuse and have different environmental conditions depending on whether they are located deep in the soil or close to the surface. A guest can always find ideal surroundings in an ant's home. In fact the greater the ant population, the larger the nest and the more suitable corners there are for guests to live in. Therefore it is the biggest and oldest ant nests that have the greater numbers of lodgers; a well established leaf-cutting ant nest (5–10 years) can be a home to around 19 species of rover beetle (Stapylinidae); even bivouacs of the nomadic army ants may be home to around 4,000 adult flies (Phorid flies).

Other species that exploit ants may not actually live inside the nest but scavenge for food on the foraging trails close by. One beetle (*Amphotis marginata*) remains near to the foraging route waiting for a worker of the shining black ant (*Lasius fuliginosus*) to return. The beetle then forces it to give up or regurgitate its food by tapping the ant's mouthparts with its forelegs. Many beetles are able to locate ant nests and their foraging routes by being able to detect the trail pheromones laid down by the scout ants.

Paying guests

Some lodgers pay their way by entering into a mutual, or symbiotic, relationship with the ants; the lodgers receive shelter and protection from predators and parasitoids which will not enter the ant nest. In return the ants obtain from the guests certain body secretions like honey-dew. The paying guests are the 'true guests' which include aphids and other homopterous bugs (insects that suck plant sap). Now, instead of the aphids living on plant stems, they live in the underground galleries of the nest where they feed on the juices of plant roots. The honey-dew they give up to the ants. If the nest is disturbed the workers rush about, pick up the aphids and carry them to safety as they do their own brood. Aphid eggs are found in the nests during the winter and the ants care for them as if they were their own. The eggs are probably maintained on the root systems of plants, but contrary to common belief there is no evidence that ants take eggs of aphids and place them on food plants outside the nest.

Certain butterfly caterpillars (Lycaenidae) depend very much on ants. Caterpillars of the European large blue butterfly (*Maculinea arion*), which is

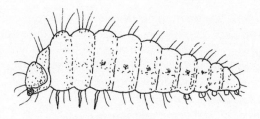

before adoption

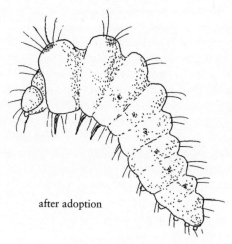

after adoption

Change in shape of the blue butterfly larva

rare in the British Isles, feeds initially on thyme until the final moult (4th larval stage) before they change into the pupae. The thyme grows on grasslands in the vicinity of red ant nests (*Myrmica*). When a red worker ant makes contact with a caterpillar the ant licks it. The caterpillar responds by changing shape: it swells, hunches up and looks completely headless. The ant then picks up the caterpillar and carries it back to its nest. In another species of the Lycaenidae, the scarce large blue (*Maculinea telejus*), the caterpillar finds and enters the ant nest by following the pheromone trails of worker ants.

In the nest the caterpillars are groomed and fed by the workers. Here they find security from parasitoids and predators. In return the caterpillars secrete, from a honey gland in the abdomen, a substance that is rich in sugar, protein and amino acids on which the ants feed. The caterpillars are covered by a large number of structures which look like tentacles; when magnified, they are rather odd shapes and can actually retract inside the caterpillar's body. These tentacles are thought to produce secretions which attract the ants. It has been suggested that these structures are actually to deter the ants from attacking the caterpillars by producing secretions which appease them. In fact, the caterpillars are sheep in wolves' clothing, for they feed on the ant larvae and homopterous insect guests residing.

When the large blue caterpillars reach maturity they pupate. The pupa stays in the ant nest over winter and continues to appease its host by producing secretions. When the adult butterfly emerges in June it is not attacked by the ants but is assisted out of the nest by the workers.

Some beetles are also true guests of ants. The following are associated with British and European ants. *Atemeles* spends most of its life in the brood chambers where it can obtain the richest supply of food – the food that is given to the ant brood. *Atemeles* spends the summer, as larvae, hosted by a *Formica* species of ant. The adult beetles then migrate to nests of *Myrmica* to spend the winter. The beetles move back to *Formica* nests in spring and summer when mating occurs. The eggs are laid with the eggs of *Formica* and when they hatch they are licked and fed by the workers as if they were one of their own. The adult beetle can stimulate the worker ant to feed it by stroking the ant's jaw with its front leg. In addition it may feed on the ant's prey, dead ants, ant eggs or larvae.

Unlike *Atemeles,* the beetle *Lomechusa* spends its entire life with the same host, the red slave-making ant (*Formica sanguinea*). The adult beetles are viviparous – giving birth to live young. The larvae are laid with the eggs of the ants and they mimic the behaviour of the ant larvae. The ants feed the beetle larvae and at any sign of danger they are the first to be carried to safety. Life gets a little more problematic for *Lomechusa* when it comes the time for the ants to spin the cocoon and the *Formica* larvae are buried by the

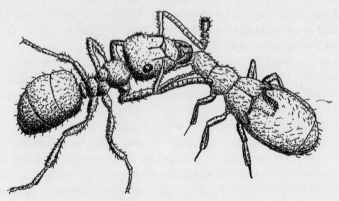

Lasius niger *feeding* claviger testaceus *beetle*

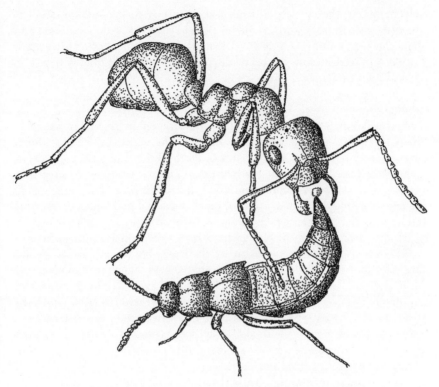

Rover beetle offering an appeasement substance to worker

workers. Both beetle and ant pupae are buried but are dug up again and moved to drier chambers. This is fine for the ant pupae but not *Lomechusa*, which cannot live in dry conditions; all the beetle larvae that get dug up die. In fact it is amazing that any survive – and only due to the oversight of the workers, who fail to dig up all the pupae.

Many of these so called 'true guests' can be rather unpleasant and you may wonder why the ants bother to invite them in the first place! One answer is that most of the beetles have very good chemical defence systems that could be used against the ants should they raise an objection. Secondly, they mimic the behaviour of ants to fool the workers into feeding them. It is likely, however, that the ants receive some nutritious secretions from the beetles. Another rover beetle (*Dinarda*) which lives in wood ant nests helps itself to food as it is being regurgitated from one worker to another. The worker ants often are covered in tiny mites and *Dinarda* grazes over the surface of the ant's body and removes them; although not a particularly welcome guest, the beetle performs a good service to the ants. Should the ants decide to attack *Dinarda*, the beetle raises the tip of the abdomen and offers the ant an appeasing droplet of fluid to keep the peace. However, if passive appeasement fails the beetle then releases a pungent fluid which soon sends the ant on its way!

Squatters

Numerous animals that live in ant nests are completely ignored by the ants. This is probably because they have acquired the odour of the ants themselves. These lodgers, all in Britain, include moths (Microlepidoptera), crickets, cockroaches, beetles (including ladybirds), flies, bugs, springtails, silverfish, spiders, false scorpions, mites, woodlice and millipedes. They are mainly scavengers eating dead ants, ant droppings, pieces of prey collected by ants and plant material from which the nest is constructed. The silverfish feeds by stealing droplets of regurgitated food as it is passed between workers.

When a wood ant's nest is disturbed there may be, as well as angry wood ants, a flutter of tiny yellowish moths from the nest. The female moth enters one of the nest chambers to lay eggs, without being attacked by the ants. Her eggs hatch into tiny caterpillars which feed on the vegetation from which the nest is built. The caterpillars build little cases from the nest material and fasten the pieces together with silk. The cases protect the caterpillars from the ants. The caterpillars overwinter in the ant nest and pupate in early summer, adults emerging at the end of June.

There are squatter ants that live in the nests of other ants; one such squatter lives in the nests of British and European wood ants. This is a tiny ant, much smaller than the wood ants themselves, called *Formicoxenus nitidulus*. The wood ants take no notice of these little fellows and leave them in peace. They probably feed on the debris inside the nest and build their own nest within the wood ants' nest from tiny bits of debris. The males are wingless but the young queens are winged. There is no nuptial flight and mating occurs inside the wood ant nest. The wings on the queens are probably a means to disperse mated queens to other wood ant nests. When the wood ants move house, as they sometimes do (see p.43), *Formicoxenus* picks up its brood and follows the wood ants.

The false scorpion is a frequent guest of wood ants but does not interfere with the ants. It also lives outside the nests in the leaf litter on the woodland floor. Spiders are common in ant nests, mostly doing the ants no harm. Woodlice live in the nests of numerous species of ants, and millipedes are particularly associated with those species that nest beneath flat stones.

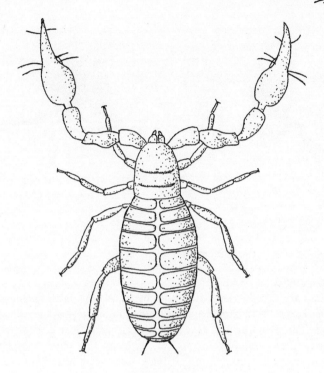

False scorpion

TRAIL FOLLOWING GUESTS

In Belgium, entomologists showed how the shining black ant (*Lasius fuliginosus*) is pursued on its foraging trail by a rover beetle (*Homoeusa acuminata*). The ants are followed for up to 20 metres (65 feet) from the nest. Most of the time the ants ignore the beetles as they run with them. A count made of the beetles along the ant trails were about two beetles every 50 cm (20 inches) but the numbers get less with distance from the nest. Scientific studies have shown that the beetles are able to detect and follow artificial extracts made from the abdominal glands of workers which lay scent trails. They usually rob the ants of their prey; however, this particular beetle has the habit of hitching a ride on the item of prey as it is being transported by the ant. It probably eats the prey as it is carried along but it may be a means of getting into the ants' nests where it tends to feed on dead ants or their food.

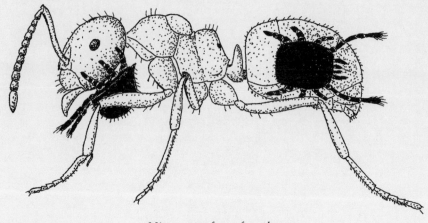

Mites on surface of workers

Unwelcome guests

Other guests are not welcomed by ants because they cause harm, offering nothing in return. Many feed on the eggs, larvae, pupae and the workers themselves. The ants can do very little about such hostile guests because these lodgers have very good defence mechanisms of a chemical nature.

A European beetle (not Britain), *Pella*, is one such guest the ants could do without. The beetle lurks inside the tunnels of the shining black ant (*Lasius fuliginosus*) where it pounces on individual workers and eventually decapitates them. The successful beetle is soon joined by other *Pella* beetles in a great feast. If the beetle is opposed then it uses its chemical defence, one of the chemicals in its armoury being very similar to the alarm pheromone produced by the ants, which causes mass panic among the ants, enabling the beetle to make its escape.

Some flies parasitise ants by laying their eggs inside them. A tiny Phorid fly (*Metopina pachycondyla*) in Texas, USA, is parasitic on the brood of a Ponerine ant (*Pachycondyla harpax*). The fly larva wraps itself around the neck of the ant larva, being held in place by small suckers. The fly larva then steals the food being fed to the ant larva. If no food reaches the fly larva then it bites the ant larva to make it wriggle until the workers bring more food. A European (not in Britain) Tachinid fly (*Strongygaster globula*) deposits its eggs inside the queen of the black garden ant. The queen is punctured with a special spine on the fly's abdomen so that the eggs may be deposited inside her. The queen ant is unable to produce her own eggs and the fly larva emerges from the queen's anus. This of course kills her and the fly larva is fed and groomed by the worker ants. The fly pupates in the ants' nest and when it hatches, not surprisingly, it makes a quick exit!

Most mites are also unwelcome for they are ectoparasites and live on the body of individual ants. A single ant may have many mites gripping onto it. One mite (*Macrocheles rettenmeyeri*) sucks the ant's blood through the thin membranes between the body segments. It also migrates to the head end and steals food when passed by mouth from one worker to another. These mites are not harmed by the ants because they have the same chemical odour as the colony; possibly they acquired it by drinking the ants' bodily fluids.

Many hostile spiders actually live just outside the nest. *Theridion riparium*, rare in Britain, is one that suspends itself by a silken thread and drops onto workers as they leave the nest to forage. The spider's lair is full of the corpses of worker ants. *Asargena phalerata* is a spider found on British heathland that preys on red ants, living in the nest entrance of the red ants, and catching them by throwing strands of silk at them with its rear legs. The unfortunate ant is then carried to the spider's lair in some corner of the ant nest and eaten.

Guests that mimic ants

Some of the guests that live with ants actually resemble ants in their body form. Beetles that run with the African driver ants are a good example. They have a slim ant-like body with a waist and petiole. For example the beetle *Mimanomma spectrum* closely resembles *Dorylus nigricans*; there are many others. It was suggested by Wasmann that ant look-a-likes evolved so that they would deceive their hosts and be accepted into the ant colony. How-

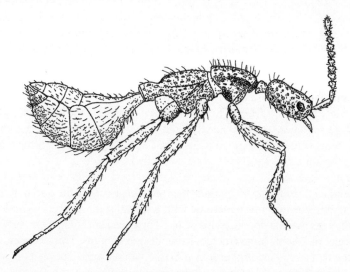

Ecitosius gracilis, a rover beetle that mimics its host ant, a New World army ant

ever, many guests are integrated into the ant society without looking like ants, they have simply acquired the colony scent. One example is a scarabid beetle (*Myrmecaphodius excavaticollis*), which moves in with fire ants. The beetle procures a coat of hydrocarbon compounds which have the odour of the species of fire ant that it is lodging with; if the beetle decides to move, it is able to shed the old coat to obtain the chemical odour of the new species of fire ant with which it wishes to move in, and successfully invade the colony.

If seems more likely that ant mimics have evolved as protection from predators outside the nest. Many of the insects that are flushed out from the vegetation by raiding army ants fall prey to birds, but those beetles that resemble ants are ignored by birds as they run with the stream of army ants.

Ants and us

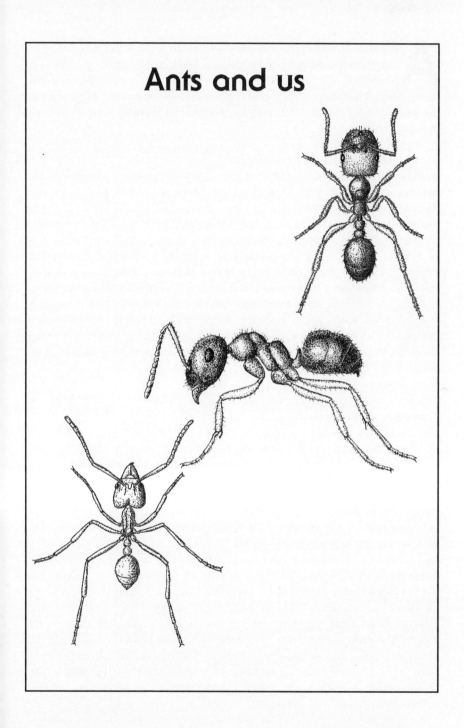

Although humans pay little attention to ants, the times when they do take notice tend to be when they view the ants as pests or carriers of human disease. Fortunately there are very few species that fall into these categories and most species are essential to cycling of soil nutrients and the protection of the environment from other insect pests. Some even serve as human food!

Ants as pests of agriculture and forestry

In some parts of the world ants are a major problem, costing millions in crop damage and pest control. However perhaps we should consider why ants became a pest species in the first place. Basically, it is the result of man's exploitation of the environment, providing ants with good food resources by planting monocultures (growing one type of plant only) of the kinds of plant that some ants like. Leaf-cutting ants, for example, under natural conditions are fussy about the type of leaves they cut; some leaves contain substances that are poisonous. The destruction of the rainforest in South America and subsequent commission of the land for agriculture has provided the ants with agricultural varieties which have had no time to evolve chemical or physical defence mechanisms against the ants. In South America the leaf-cutting ants are a major economic problem damaging forestry, particularly eucalyptus and pine plantations, destruction of agricultural crops, citrus plantations and stored products. The leaf-cutting ants are able to strip a citrus tree of all its leaves over night. In some plantations there may be 20–30 nests per hectare of land and loss may run as high as 50%. The leaf-cutting ants also cause structural damage to roads in Brazil; where they build their nests beneath the Trans-Amazon highway the tarmac is weakened, consequently trucks often fall into huge craters created by a large nest built at the edge of the road.

In the USA fire ants are a major pest. The great fire ant invasion in the 1920s caused damage to agriculture throughout the United States, and the ants now infest approximately 100 million hectares of land in 11 states. The ants, which are reddish-brown to black (workers 2–6 mm and queens 7–8 mm long), are found from Arizona and California to the southern states, Texas to South Carolina. The most notorious is the imported red fire ant (*Solenopsis invicta*). As the name suggests, these were imported from a supply ship which arrived at Port Mobile about 76 years ago from South America. They cause most damage to crops but kill citrus trees by chewing the bark around the base of the trunk. Between 1957 and 1981 the United States spent over $172 million on the control of fire ants. In India fire ants are a major pest of spice crops, cucumber, tomato, banana, mango and citrus. Damage to stored silk worm cocoons is estimated at 50–60% loss. Another

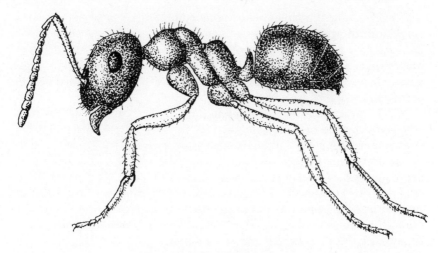

Lasius niger, *a domestic ant*

species of the same genus, the thief ant, is a pest of strawberries and vegetables; in addition it is the intermediate host of a poultry tapeworm.

Other pests ants include the Argentine ant (*Iridomyrmex humilis*), native of South America but well established in the USA. This species is carnivorous but attacks stored products, fruit and figs. The harvester ants (*Pogonomyrmex*) are also a cause for concern in the United States. They prefer to nest in open sunny locations around farmland where they cause agricultural losses through their habit of foraging on crop or pasture seeds. In Australia it was found that nearly all the seed that is sown (about 10 kg of seed per hectare) may be removed within 16 hours by the harvester ant *Pheidole*. In Britain ants are not usually thought of as serious pests of agriculture, but some are considered pests of gardens, particularly because of their habit of harbouring aphids and other bugs (see p.49).

Ants as domestic pests

Owing to the improvement of domestic heating systems, many buildings have become inhabited by an immigrant ant from Egypt. The pharaoh ant (*Monomorium pharaonis*) invades blocks of flats, hospitals, bakeries and office blocks. The ant is very tiny, no more than 2 mm, and is able to build its nest in tiny cracks in the plaster, behind electrical sockets, ducting, even inside vending machines. In fact, it makes its nest in the most inaccessible places which makes it very difficult to eradicate. Winged queens and males are produced but there is no nuptial flight, mating takes place inside the nest. Each nest has hundreds of queens and thousands of workers; the queens lay around 35 eggs per day which amounts to about 4,500 eggs in a queen's lifetime. When the nest gets too large smaller nests are budded from the main nest and moved to new sites. The ants do not bite or sting but their jaws are capable of chewing rubber and cloth. The major hazard of these ants is the spread of disease (p.115).

Black garden ants are often found indoors because they usually make nests very close to buildings and beneath the foundations. Black ants may enter a house from the outside through a tiny crack in the plaster or under the door. A blob of jam or a few crumbs of cake will be enough for a scout ant to recruit its nest mates to the food inside the house. Occasionally a close relative of the black garden ant *Lasius brunneus* will nest within oak timbers of older houses. These ants can cause structural damage to timbers particularly where the wood is damp. They will eat their way into the rotting timber and into new timbers as well as making a nest.

Control of ants

Chemical control of ants is very expensive because it is labour intensive, requiring skilled workers; the methods used to control leaf-cutting ants in South America are mainly chemical, although dynamiting the nests has been attempted. Chemicals include fumigation of the nests with cyanide gas, a very hazardous procedure, and the use of organochlorine compounds which are pumped into the nests. The most successful is mirex – a stomach poison – added to a bait. The problems with these compounds is that they are highly toxic to all animal life and persist in the environment for a very long time. Recent research is now trying to come up with environmentally safe methods. Biological control includes infecting ants with a fungus which will kill them.

Fire ants are still a major problem and the use of mirex has been banned in the USA. New methods include toxic baits (pellets of puffed cereals, corn, wheat or rice) which are taken into the nest by foraging workers. Baits usually incorporate an attractant to encourage the ants to pick up the bait. Recent research is concentrating on using pheromones to attract the fire ants to baits. Minced liver is used as a bait to control the pharaoh ant. The bait is laced with a synthetic hormone and when it is taken back to the nest by the workers, the hormone prevents the queens from reproducing. This method is preferred over spraying, particularly in operating theatres where insecticidal spray would be dangerous. However, these ants to date have proved difficult to eradicate and cause serious problems in hospitals.

The synthetic insect hormones used against fire ants are very effective but they are slow acting because they do not instantly destroy the ants, only prevent further generations of ants from being born. Other methods which are less effective are insecticides, such as sprays, powders, or granules, which must come into contact with the ants. In the case of fire ants the insecticide is applied to the nest; the trouble is that if all the ants are not completely killed they will just move to another location. It has been found that treating seeds before sowing with dieldrin will reduce the amount of seeds foraged by harvester ants, although the use of baits incorporating insecticides is more effective.

For those that have domestic problems with black garden ants indoors the old fashion environmentally friendly – but not very ant friendly – method of pouring boiling water on the nest outside is probably the best. I did hear recently of an ant friendly method of deterring ants from entering the house, which is to put a large tin of syrup outside in the garden; the ants find this a far more attractive proposition, and it is probably cheaper than a chemical! It is better to use the preventive technique of making sure that there is no food source present for the ants inside the house. And don't forget that ants do a good job of removing all our organic litter in towns. There are many commercial sprays and powders available for dealing with ants but these are expensive and usually toxic to humans or pets and ecologically unsafe. For those species of ants that have invaded wooded structural supports of a house it is far better to seek professional advice as the timbers may need replacing.

LEAF-CUTTING ANTS IMPROVE SOIL

Recent research has shown that leaf-cutting ants are important in improving the fertility of the soil, particularly where the primary forest in Brazil has been felled. Scientist dug holes 5 metres deep in the middle of ant nests to collect soil samples. These samples when compared to samples taken in similar forests, with no ants, are in much better condition. Soils taken from the nests are very crumbly which makes it easy for plant roots to grow through. The leaf-cutting ant nests have chambers which contain unwanted leaf fragments and as these leaf pieces rot away they make the soil less acidic. This enables soil to hold onto plant nutrients longer making them more fertile. In acid soil these nutrients are soon washed out.

Garden ants: friend or foe?

Ecologically speaking, gardens provide ideal habitats for ants, especially where a wide diversity of natural vegetation grows. A diversity of vegetation means there will be more insect life for food and nest sites. Gardens are normally sheltered and usually receive plenty of sunlight which is attractive to ants.

Unfortunately, ants may not be too popular with some gardeners. Black ants are known to damage seedlings possibly by chewing through the roots as part of their digging behaviour. They will eat the caruncle, or small swelling on the seed, of *Viola* and *Primula* seeds, which is very rich in oil. However, the seed will continue to germinate, so the ants are probably an important agent of seed dispersal. It might be a good idea not to sow seeds in the vicinity of ant nests.

Red ants are very fond of soft fruit and will chew into the flesh of strawberries and raspberries, which does not endear them to gardeners; nor does their habit of 'farming' aphids for honey-dew. The ants protect aphids from predators so numbers can build up, also aphid colonies that are tended by ants produce larger volumes of honey-dew than those aphids which are not ant tended. Aphids stay on the plant longer when ants are present; the production of winged aphids (which normally fly away) is prevented by a pheromone substance produced by the ants themselves.

These are the bad points; but I feel that their good points outweigh the bad. Plants become infested by aphids whether or not ants are on the plants. Quite often plants become sticky with honey-dew which permits mould to grow and cuts down the amount of light reaching the leaves. Ants will clean up any excess honey-dew and remove any aphid skins stuck in the honey-dew after a moult. The greatest benefits of ants in gardens is the destruction of garden pests. The foraging ants will kill small larvae of various flies, sawflies and moths, wire worms, mites, springtails and large populations of aphids, for when aphid populations get too large ants will 'cull' them. In greenhouses black garden ants help to reduce pests.

Foraging ants cover large areas in the search for food. The hunting grounds of ants from different colonies may overlap. Black ants may travel 3 metres (10 feet) from their nests and red ants might travel 8 metres (26 feet). Red ants are capable of killing at least 40% of a proportion of newly hatched plant-feeding bugs and 30% of fly populations. Owing to an extremely high intake of food to feed developing brood in the nests, ants are among the most efficient invertebrate predators.

Ants help to pollinate flowers by feeding on the sweet nectar. Their tunnelling behaviour improves soil structure where the soil is compact and hard. Ants also increase the amount of organic matter which is mixed with the subsoil in the same way that earthworms do. Therefore they are particularly important in acidic soils which are unsuitable for earthworms. Soil acidity may also be slightly reduced by the tunnelling activity of ants. The yellow meadow ant is responsible for building ant-hills in old lawns. This results in a small mound of earth which eventually dries up to leave a crumbly top soil. This renders the soil highly porous to air and water, essential for the growth of grass.

Remember, gardens that are organically cultivated, without the use of chemical sprays, are likely to have a greater variety of ant species; the activities of ants might have further advantages to the gardener yet to be discovered.

Ants as biological control agents

Ants were the first insects to be used as a natural means to control pests. In Yemen ants brought down from the mountains have been used to kill the ants that plagued the date groves. In south China green tree ants are placed in the citrus groves to rid the trees of pests.

Ants are a far more effective control method than any chemicals. Various species have been studied for their potential as biological control agents. In North America, wood ants are used to control a moth larva known as the spruce budworm (*Choristoneura*) which is capable of defoliating spruce trees. A serious outbreak could cost many acres of forest. The budworm hibernate during the winter in little silk cocoons which are concealed in the needle shaped leaves of the spruce. The larvae emerge in the spring and feed on the young shoots. A single nest of wood ants can destroy between 5,000–12,000 budworm larvae each day. Wood ants also kill winter moth larvae which attack oak, gypsy moth larvae, larch sawfly larvae and various insects that damage pine trees.

Wood ants were found to be highly favourable for pest control as they are fairly large (up to 9.5 mm in length) and aggressive and nests contain large numbers. A single nest might house between 100,000 and 400,000 workers, plus 100 or so queens. They have been used successfully to counteract pest outbreaks in forests of Europe and North America. Wood ants are able to respond rapidly to pest outbreaks and deal with them quickly. Foraging wood ants from a single nest can destroy 20,000 insects in one day, more than half these being pest species. Thousands of wood ant nests have been transplanted to forests, which have no wood ants, in Italy and Spain to thwart forest pests.

Ants and human disease

Generally, ants are not considered as carriers of human disease. However there is one exception: the pharaoh ant, because of its habit of nesting in hospitals (p.111). The g ant has been found to carry at least twenty types of pathogenic bacteria which can be transmitted to humans. These bacteria include *Staphylococcus, Streptococcus, Pseudomonas, Clostridium,* and *Salmonella.*

Ants have a real affinity for protein as well as sweet sugary substances and they are not fussy from where they obtain their food – be it dustbins, drains, or lesions on patients in hospital. As the pharaoh ant is very small it

WELL, THEY'RE ON **SPECIAL OFFER** THIS WEEK

can crawl beneath bandages and dressing, which are normally sterile, and feed from wounds. The food and bacteria imbibed by the ants may be regurgitated from worker to worker, which spreads bacteria to other patients. The ants can contaminate sterile dressings, syringe needles, catheters, glucose and plasma bags as they are fed into patients. The pharaoh ant is not only a nuisance but a serious vector of human disease.

Another ant which is a threat to human life but does not really cause a disease is the fire ant because of its painful sting. When the ant stings it injects venom which causes a burning sensation – hence the name fire ants. A few hours later the skin blisters and after 24 hours the blisters become full of liquid as the tissue begins to digest as a result of the action by the venom. There is always the possibility of infection but more serious is that some people develop an allergic reaction and can die if they do not receive medical treatment. About 1,460 cases of fire ant allergy are reported every year in the USA.

Ants as food for humans

Army ant queens, known as 'sausage ants', are eaten by various tribes. The Australian aborigines are very partial to honey ants. These ants store food in their crop normally to feed the rest of the colony (p.51). In the crop, a brownish liquid consists mainly of sugar – glucose and fructose, so honey ants are very sweet, just like candy!

Locals in South America eat the abdomens of the leaf-cutting ant queens, which are probably very nutritious due to being full of eggs. The abdomens are either eaten raw, roasted or fried – take your pick. In the United States they are even canned! I have been told that they taste like shrimps and are very nice, but bits of insect cuticle (outer integument) are difficult to get out from between the teeth!

ANTS AS INDICATORS OF POLLUTION

Wood ants may be useful as biological indicators of air pollution by heavy metals like lead, cadmium, copper and zinc. Wood ants collect large quantities of honey-dew from aphids, who imbibe plant sap which is contaminated. The heavy metals enter the plant tissues as the plants 'breathe' polluted air. In industrial areas where pollution levels are high wood ants living in the surrounding countryside have been found to contain large quantities of heavy metals. The pollutants have been found in the brood as well as the adults. Curiously, wood ants appear to be highly resistant to such pollutants and are able to survive for a long time in environments polluted with heavy metals.

Should we help conserve them?

In short the answer is – yes. Owing to increasing pressure on the land caused by expansion of cities and towns, intensive agriculture involving pesticides, exploitation of forests for timber production (particularly where deciduous woodland is being replaced by conifer species) ants and many other insects are under threat. Wood ants are exploited by pheasant and fish farmers who dig over the nests to steal the brood for bird or fish food. Even careless walkers who stir up a wood ant nest with a stick do not realise the harm they cause by destroying the nest structure which maintains the optimal temperature inside for the development of the brood. Many of the recreational activities enjoyed by human beings can cause harm to wildlife. In Germany, Switzerland, Belgium and Luxemburg wood ants are protected by law because of the good they do.

In Britain, there are several species of wood ant now threatened with extinction. In Scotland, around Glen Lyon, only a small number of nests of a rather sluggish wood ant, the Scottish wood ant (*Formica aquilonia*), remain. The decline of this species is due to heavy grazing of scrub, preventing the regeneration of dense woodland in which *Formica aquilonia* thrives. The dense plantations of spruce in Scotland are totally unsuitable for wood ants because hardly any light reaches the forest floor beneath them; very few plants are able to grow here, and consequently fewer insects, and no food for the wood ants. It has been suggested that wood ants require certain species of aphids (important to the ants because they produce honey-dew which is a food source (p.49); these aphids cannot survive in conifer plantations. Furthermore, in order to colonise new areas wood ants may require an abundance of other ant species to assist them in founding new colonies (see p.42)

Other species of ants in Britain, related to wood ants, are on the decline. *Formica pratensis* was until recently found in a small area close to the south coast (Dorset). It is now extinct. Fortunately, it still survives in Europe. The narrow-headed ant *(Formica exsecta)* is also endangered. In England only a few colonies exist, in Devon. This species has been driven out largely by the red wood ant *(Formica rufa)* which is a more successful competitor. However, the red wood ant cannot take all the blame. Red wood ants are able to colonise wood and scrub which has encroached onto heathland where *Formica exsecta* lives. *Formica exsecta* prefers more open land like heaths, woodland rides and glades; without proper land management these areas become overgrown, which is fine for the red wood ant but spells doom for *Formica exsecta*. If this species is to survive, the Devon heathland must be managed properly to maintain it in a semi-natural state. In addition many of the nests on the Devon heaths are being destroyed by human activities such as motorcycle scrambling which churn up the ground and the nests! Fortunately, *Formica exsecta* stills survives near the Cairngorms – for the moment.

OBSERVING ANTS IN A FORMICARIUM

Ants are far more interesting when observed alive. They can be kept in a formicarium which can be made from any large plastic container such as a lunch box or ice cream carton. Into the box place several test tubes covered with silver foil to keep out the light. The ants will use these tubes as nests. An extra tube filled half way with water and plugged with cotton wool will keep the container moist. On the bottom of the container place a piece of paper towel or cotton wool soaked in honey water (1 part honey to 10 parts water) as an energy source. Remember ants need protein so provide them with freshly killed insects. Finally, dust the edges of the box with talcum powder to prevent the ants from escaping over the sides. You are now ready to collect your ants. Garden ants are easy to maintain, just dig up a nest and collect as many workers as possible with a damp paint brush. Try also to collect the queens who will continue to lay eggs. The formicarium will require some looking after by removing uneaten insects and replacing fresh honey water and topping up the water reservoir.

Not only in Britain are ants and other insects endangered. *Nothomyrmecia macrops,* considered to be a 'living fossil' because it was thought to be extinct in Western Australia, was rediscovered alive and well in 1977 near Ceduna, South Australia. This very primitive ant lives in small populations beneath *Eucalyptus* trees in dense forest. It navigates by using the pattern of the tree canopy above its nest (see p.81). If the trees are cut down it is not able to find its way around and eventually dies out. Although *Nothomyrmecia* is of value to collectors, a serious threat to its existence is land development. The site near Ceduna was destroyed because of the installation of an underground telephone line. Most of the *Nothomyrmecia* population has been wiped out. Other nearby sites are known and are under close watch by people who want to save them.

About half the species of ants in Holland are endangered, rare or extinct, and the remaining species have declined due to human activities, agriculture and pollution. Acid rain makes heathland plants more vulnerable to frost damage, the heaths are then more susceptible to invasion by grasses, bracken and shrub which are detrimental to certain species of ants which live on heaths. Excessive manuring of grassland renders the land uninhabitable by ants.

Ants have an important role to play in the ecosystem by interacting with other organisms and the physical environment. Further they are a good indicator species of a stable environment; the more species of ants present in an area of woodland or grassland, the greater will be the diversity of other plants and animals. Overall, remember each ant species is an important part of our British fauna and it would be a pity to lose any of them.

THE RETURN OF THE LARGE BLUE BUTTERFLY

The large blue butterfly spends 10 months of its life inside an ant's nest. The female large blue lays her eggs on the common thyme and when the caterpillars hatch they feed on the flowers. After the caterpillars have finished their final moult they are taken into a nest by red ants where they are fed and cared for until they emerge as adult butterflies.

In 1979 the large blue became extinct in Britain. This was because the butterfly depends totally on one species of red ant (*Myrmica sabuleti*). The population of red ants declined as the grasslands in which they build their nests became cooler: the grass was no longer being grazed by rabbits and sheep and so grew taller and shaded the nests. No ants – no butterflies, it was as simple as that. In order to reintroduce the large blue the ants had to return to the grassland. This meant that the land had to be managed properly by periodic mowing or grazing. The reintroduction scheme of the large blue has been successful in a few nature reserves, provided they are managed, which is costly. Now the tide has turned. Due to global warming the soil of many grasslands which are not managed, is reaching a much higher temperature, equivalent to that of managed grassland, so now it seems likely that the ants and the large blue butterfly could return to those grasslands from where they originally became extinct.

Further reading

H. St. J. K . Donisthorpe, *The guests of British ants* (George Routledge & Sons Ltd, London, 1927)

J. H. Sudd, *An introduction to the behaviour of ants* (Edward Arnold Ltd, London, 1967)

E.O. Wilson, *The Insect Societies* (The Belkan Press of Harvard University Press, Cambridge, Massachusetts, 1972)

M.V. Brian, *Ants* (Collins, London, 1977)

J.H. Sudd & N.R Franks, *The behavioural ecology of ants* (Blackie, London & Glasgow, 1987)

B. Hölldobler & E. O. Wilson, *The Ants* (The Belkan Press of Harvard University Press, Cambridge, Massachusetts, 1990)

Research and Survey in Nature Conservation, no 35: *A review of the scarce and threatened bees, wasps and ants of Great Britain (*Nature Conservancy Council, 1991)

Index

figures in bold indicate illustrations

red garden ants 11, 26, 30, 36, 39,54, 65, 82, 89
red slave-making ant 97, 98, 102
reproduction 13, 33, 34, 43, 45
rhythms 37
Rhytidoponera 40
rover beetle 100, **103**, 105

scent trails 77, 79, 80, 86, 89, 95, 105
slaves 5, 94, 97, 98
social insects 8, 13, 19, 26
soil improvement 113
soldier ants 19, 84
Solenopsis 11, 19, 82, 86, 91, 110
Sphecomyrma 16
spiders 88, 92, 100, 104, 107
spruce budworm 115
sting 11, 28, 29, 30, 40, 54, 84, 88, 89, 90, 91, 96, 112, 116
Strongylognathus 96, 97
sub-castes 19

temperature 17, 33, 36, 38, 41, 61, 63, 64, 65, 66, 69, 73, 75, 117, 120
temporary social parasitism 42

termites 8, 10, 46, 82
territory 28, 84, 85, 86
Tetramorium 96, 97
Teleutomyrmex 96
Theridion 107
thief ant 91, 95, 111
thorax 8, 19, 27, 40, 57
Tiphiidae 15
trophallaxis 50

viola 26, 114

wall-papering ant 75
wasps 8, 11, 14, 15, 16, 17, 24, 54, 61, 82, 88
weaver ants 12, 71, 74, 84, 85
Wilson, Ernest 8, 16
wood ants 12, 13, 22, 26, 27, 35, 37, 38, 39, 40, 41, 43, 49, 50, 54, 55, 61, 62, 63, 69, 77, 80, 82, 84, 91, **92**, 93, 97, 104, 115, 117, 118
woodlice 100, 104

Zacryptocerus 87, 88

If you have enjoyed this book, you might be interested in other natural history titles we publish; write for a free booklist to 18 Anley Road, London W14 OBY. You may purchase the titles below either from bookshops or direct from us. All are priced at £7.99 except where indicated, and all are illustrated with line drawings throughout. Please add £1.50 p & p when ordering direct:

World Wildlife Series

BIG CATS
Douglas Richardson
(£9.99)

CHIMPANZEES
Tess Lemmon

DOLPHINS
Peter Evans

DUCKS
David Tomlinson

PARROTS
David Alderton
(£9.99)

PENGUINS
John A. Love

SEA OTTERS
John A. Love
(£9.99)

SPIDERS
Michael Chinery

British Natural History Series

BADGERS
Michael Clark

BATS
Phil Richardson

DEER
Norma Chapman

EAGLES
John A. Love

FALCONS
Andrew Village

FROGS AND TOADS
Trevor Beebee

GARDEN CREEPY-CRAWLIES
Michael Chinery

HEDGEHOGS
Pat Morris

MAMMAL DETECTIVE
Rob Strachan

MICE AND VOLES
John Flowerdew

OTTERS
Paul Chanin

OWLS
Chris Mead

POND LIFE
Trevor Beebee

PONIES IN THE WILD
Elaine Gill

PUFFINS
Kenny Taylor

RABBITS AND HARES
Anne McBride

ROBINS
Chris Mead

SEALS
Sheila Anderson

SNAKES AND LIZARDS
Tom Langton

SQUIRRELS
Jessica Holm

STOATS AND WEASELS
Paddy Sleeman

URBAN FOXES
Stephen Harris

URBAN WILDLIFE
Peter Shirley

WHALES
Peter Evans

WILDCATS
Mike Tomkies